AF422518

FIGURE DRAWING: RHYTHM AND LANGUAGE OF THE HUMAN FORM

Volume I

Gabrielle Dahms

This is a non-fiction work.

Copyright © Booksmart Press LLC 2024

All materials, including the original drawings by Gabrielle Dahms, are copyrighted.

All opinions and remaining spelling or grammatical mistakes are those of the author.

This book or any portion of it may not be reproduced or used in any manner whatsoever without the express prior written permission of the publisher except for use of brief quotations in a book review. For permission requests, email the author at info@figuredrawing.life.

Book Cover by 100Covers

Published by Booksmart Press LLC

ISBN 13: 979-8-2302212-5-8 (paperback)

ISBN 13: 979-8-9853675-3-9 (ebook)

ISBN13: 979-8-9853675-1-5(hardcover)

Publisher's Cataloging-in-Publication Data

Names: Dahms, Gabrielle, author.

Title: Figure drawing : rhythm and language of the human form / Gabrielle Dahms.

Description: Includes bibliographical references and index. | Cheyenne, WY: BookSmart Press, 2024.

Identifiers: LCCN: 2024918992 | ISBN: 979-8-9853675-1-5 (hardcover) | 979-8-9853675-2-2 (paperback) | 979-8-9853675-3-9 (ebook)
Subjects: LCSH Human figure in art. | Drawing--Technique. | BISAC ART/ Subjects & Themes / Human Figure | ART/ Techniques / Drawing | ART/ Techniques / Life Drawing | ART/ Subjects & Themes / Portraits | ART/ Techniques / Composition
Classification: LCC NC765 .D34 2024 | DDC 743/.4--dc23

Dedication

To all outstanding teachers on whose shoulders I stand.
With special acknowledgement to Sharon Pearson
and Alan McCorkle.

Also By

Other Books by the Author

Figure Drawing Workbook: Rhythm and Language of the Human Form (Vol. II)

The Real Estate Investor Manuals

How Trends Make You A Smarter Investor (Vol. I)

Finding Profitable Deals (Vol. II)

The Art and Science of Real Estate Negotiation (Vol. III)

Investing in Real Estate in Your Self-Directed IRA (Vol. IV)

Table of Contents

Table of Figures

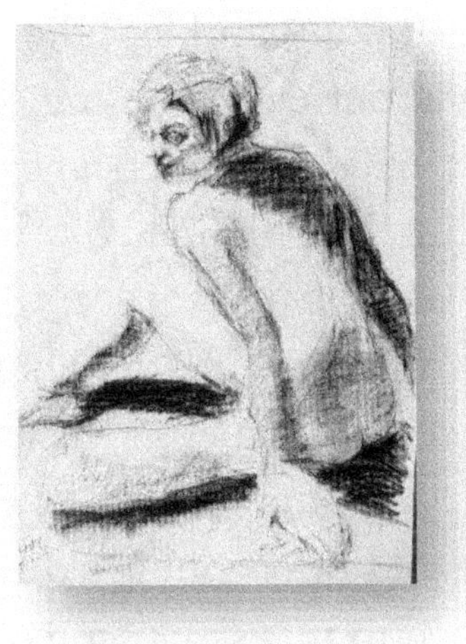

Introduction

How excellent and freeing it is to draw. And the figure at that!

You are reading these pages because drawing the figure attracts and interests you. Maybe you've always been interested in drawing, or learning how to draw. Perhaps you want to engage your creative side while pursuing a career elsewhere. Perhaps you want to pursue something completely new and drawing the figure appeals to you.

The body's language is amazing. It is a privilege to capture this, to explore it, to build on it, to respond to it. Yet, what drives me and informs me is the love of beauty. This beauty excludes the perfect ideals projected by fashion magazines, air-

1

brushed images of anything. The beauty I love is unique, makes no excuses, shows up authentically, among other things.

I prize the beauty of individuality, of self-expression, of quiet certitude, of flaunting nothing, the beauty of that which wants to be seen without ever pointing out that it exists. The beauty of seeing, learning and understanding for oneself versus that which our culture has defined as such. For me, it takes courage to do so.

The human figure is amazing to behold. It is also difficult to capture. I embrace that immense challenge.

I remember the first time I saw an original Rembrandtpainting and how connected I felt to the sitter, the model in it. I returned to that painting repeatedly at the Legion of Honor museum in San Francisco. Those returns spanned over two decades until I came to contemplate the painting one day and found it was on loan to another museum.

The painting, a portrait of a Dutch nobleman who had commissioned Rembrandt, always spoke to me. Eventually, I realized that the humanity, the psychological accuracy in it, transcends all time. Of course, many other artists inspire me.

My desire to draw goes as far back as I can remember, perhaps because drawing seemed a way to bring body, mind and spirit together. That first desire was not specific to drawing the figure.

Then, I was a poor draughts woman, and I had no training and no idea how to draw anything accurately and well. That would wait for at least another two decades, and then I was only beginning. As the saying goes, no one knows what he or she doesn't know. I was no exception.

Once this became apparent, distress set in because I just believed I ought to be able to draw. Isn't that what many of us have been told? It's easy. Anyone can draw. As I dug deeper and sought instruction,

I realized my impatience and a certain vanity. I wanted my drawings to look good and to be praised for them, and hear that line: "oh, you are a natural artist."

I was far from embodying any of that, and trying to reconcile all that made my drawing journey more difficult. It took me years to overcome the vanity affliction. That probably came through the process of putting in endless hours of practice, studying the Masters, reading, and absorbing the fundamentals. There is no room for vanity or even impatience when doing all that.

Drawing the figure is observation in action, the creation of an expression of what is in front of me, of the world as a microcosm, and again of what's inside. Drawing, and especially drawing the figure, enables any serious artist to become conscious. And every drawing journey differs from the next, for you, for me, for any artist.

What you already know, engage, and experience in your life flows into any drawing, mostly unseen until excelling in all fundamental drawing skills.

This body is an amazing instrument and when I see the figure in front of me or even in my mind's eye, a magnetic force compels me to observe, express, record - and finally to let go of it all. Perhaps what's on the paper in the end is an internal release of sorts. While none of this is technical, the process of what I just described informs my drawing more than I ever realized. And the technical stuff connected to seeing becomes increasingly more important because of it!

You might notice that in telling you a little about my drawing trajectory, there is hardly a mention of the technical details. There are many of them, naturally, and what you read here refers to them and to the artistic journey.

I could, for example, tell you about my struggles with finding the waist, with foreshortening, with anatomical accuracy, with materials and media, among many others. These are important, but when drawing the figure, learning to see trumps all. As the observer of human expressions and studying them alongside the model's attitudes, demeanor, capturing and expressing those lends any drawing vitality and force. Extraordinary technical skill coupled with artistic experimentation become its lifeblood.

If one is master of one thing and understands one thing well, one has, at the same time, insight into and understanding of many things. —Vincent Van Gogh

---

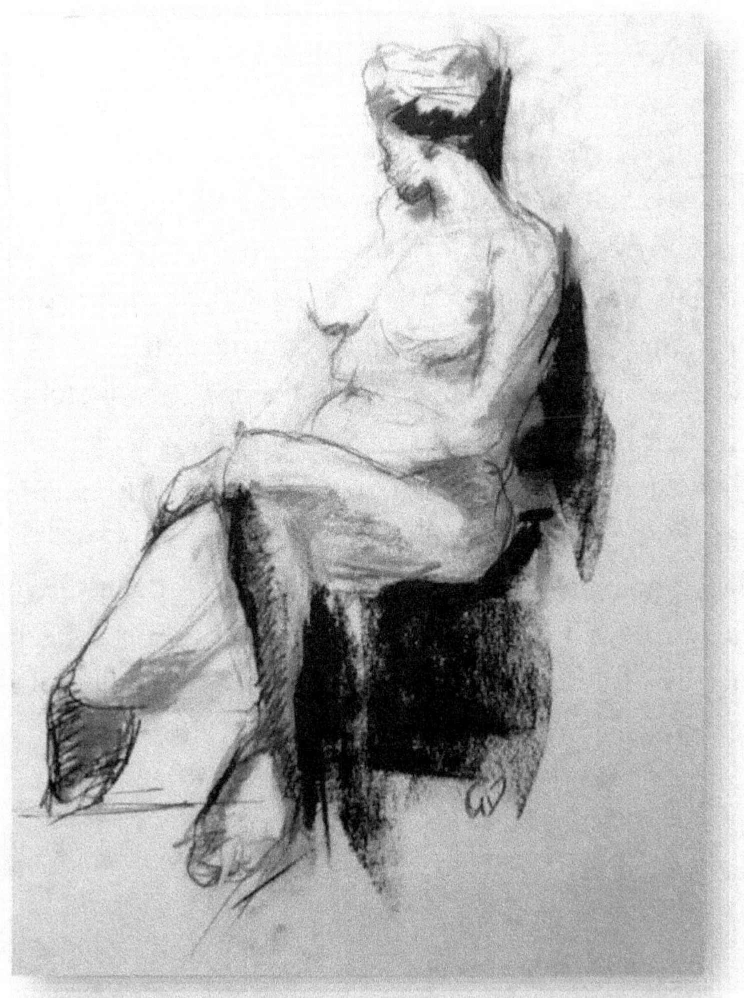

Figure 1 Seated Female

Drawing is a language, and all great art stems from learning the vocabulary and syntax. Just like with any language, those represent the fundamentals. Great artists never tire of the fundamentals because they are what affords them to express themselves. Knowing only one phrase won't do. It's akin to having a conversation when all you can say is *Hello, how are you?*

To illustrate this point, let's look at master draftsman, sculptor, and painter Michelangelo Buonarotti (1475-1564). He focused on anatomical studies and preparatory sketches.

And his beautiful works rest on his knowledge of classical and mythological sources. A true master of the Renaissance and contemporary of Leonardo DaVinci (1452-1519), Michaelangelo studied under other masters and applied himself to his work with endless energy. All his works bespeak his devotion to meticulous study and preparation. He left little to chance and his artistic expression found life and greatness via his continual work on the fundamentals.

To understand the human body is to understand the divine design of creation itself.—Michaelangelo

---

With this in mind, Michaelangelo aimed to infuse his drawings, paintings and sculptures with the pulse of life. In all his works, he worked from an initial concept, usually captured via quick lines, to refinement via detailed studies of different body parts, for example, to highly detailed but still preparatory drawings.

Imagine a young Michaelangelo drawing and sketching the ancient sculptures in Lorenzo de Medici's gardens, his fingers charcoal-stained. Lorenzo apparently caught the boy doing just that and was so impressed that he invited Michaelangelo to live in his palace and study under his patronage.

While my evolution as an artist lacked such patronage, I spent and continue to spend countless hours sketching and drawing the human figure. I love the spontaneity of drawing, yet I realized somewhere during my first five hundred hours of learning to draw that true artistic expression only happens when mastering the fundamentals.

I think of art as a language comprising vocabulary, grammar, and syntax. That may sound dry and tedious, but it can be great fun to learn all that is required.

Drawing the figure is both challenging and exhilarating. I have made many drawing mistakes. The great news is that mistakes are stepping stones to mastery. They are absolutely necessary because they deepen one's craft, so long as artists learn from them and overcome them. You will benefit from my mistakes because they are common to all aspiring artists.

Art was part of my life in my early years via mandatory art classes. Not one of these classes taught drawing and certainly not figure drawing. Instead, they pushed craft projects of which I remember an odious and tedious one that involved bunching colored paper into little balls, then gluing these balls to a paper surface. Unfortunately, I learned little about art and the whole thing invoked yawns in me. That's as far as my official art education progressed.

Still, I have drawn since my teenage years, though rather poorly in the beginning. Eventually, art classes followed and stirred a thirst to excel in drawing. The human figure always was my special interest, though the initial foray led into the land of floating heads. Fascinated by portraiture, but lacking knowledge of the fundamentals, including structure and design elements, those first results seemed good to me. Once my art education progressed, I viewed them differently, mainly as instructional road markers.

Having drawn the figure in its many aspects for almost forty years, I look back and appreciate several great instructors I had. They were few, and one thing I realized was that a person may be a great artist and a lousy teacher at the same time. This phenomenon explains many art classes in which instructors declared: *just draw what you see and have fun.*

This laissez-faire teaching attitude amounted to little or no teaching and simply babysitting the students. What a sad statement for art and for teaching!

Finding an excellent teacher is essential for engaging in the work of drawing. It can shave many years of learning the hard way. Outstanding teachers are just as rare as great artists, but they exist. Some qualities all such teachers share include focus, concentration, discipline, articulating the material well, understanding how to work with models and how to light them, and an abiding interest in their students' progress.

Never underestimate feedback from your teachers. Receive it gracefully and with gratitude, even though it might take you years to understand and appreciate it.

These teachers entice their students to become knowledgeable about art and even art history. They show what art can be, what the creative process can be.

There is nothing lackadaisical about them. They take a deep interest in their students, their abilities and their artistic development. They inspire.

They signal to their students that drawing is somatic wisdom. Drawing is also a meditation about life and sometimes about the settings and the poses you draw.

In decades of taking classes, I was fortunate to encounter two teachers of this caliber. They are the people to whom I dedicate this book. And it is what they taught me and how that melded with my abilities, and developed over decades this book contains.

Now that you know a little about my artistic journey, I briefly want to address autodidacts. It is possible to study books by eminent artists and teachers, to visit museums to immerse yourself into the art world through the ages, and to become adept at all the required aspects. However, in most times, this takes many, many years and lacks the valuable feedback needed to advance. It whittles down artistic choices in many times.

Like with all habits, establishing a routine, a process, an internal connection to the subject derives from understanding all the puzzle pieces. That means having a bigger vision than any one drawing AND employing the technical know-how and discipline necessary.

What goes into any drawing is the engagement with the model, the artist community (living and dead), and with all the topics in this book. For example, an artist's knowledge and appreciation of anatomy, of how muscles, tendons, ligaments work informs the artist's drawing, but is otherwise invisible to viewers.

Many aspiring artists and even advanced artists get stuck when teasing out what knowledge, approach, and understanding are necessary. In the words of Victor Perard,

Students may plow through many pages of text, [yet] often fail to visualize the subject properly because many textbooks contain insufficient descriptive drawings.

Perard's classic on figure drawing depicts wonderful descriptive sketches of the human figure.

While this book on figure drawing contains some descriptive drawings, it aims to bring you drawing resources to consult and study. Inspiring you to start, improve, and excel at drawing the figure is its aim.

Everyone starts at the same place and must imbibe knowledge and vision to master drawing the figure. Mastery of anything demands at least ten thousand hours of practice. **That means actual drawing.** Reading and studying may require an equal amount of hours.

This may seem intimidating. Don't let it be. Instead, get started. Every moment is precious and counts.

When drawing a human being, whether a model or a friend, doing so is a privilege.

The model is a living, breathing organism. The model moves and movement brings forth different perspectives, views, and forms and limbs that change according to these.

Distinct, sometimes contrasting emotions and attitudes also show up.

Having a model, especially one who understands how to pose and how to move, is a boon. Every model, big or small, fat or lean, muscular or flabby, male or female, contains a person's spirit, emotions, and attitudes. For that reason, every model comprises her or his own beauty. That beauty does not depend on whether you believe the model is beautiful. Drawing the model presents a surprise a day!

So, what does all this have to do with drawing from life versus from photographs?

Photographs are static representations. They hold moments in time and cannot come close to drawing a live model. Drawings from photographs have their place, but remember that they usually lack the aliveness that models bring to a pose. Photos sometimes also are too perfect, too polished. There is nothing messy about them, yet anything alive has something messy about it.

Such messiness renders the subject interesting.

Drawings from photographs also have light on them that distort the image. For example, eyes and pupils drawn from photos reflect whichever light the photographer used. Their values and what the eyes communicate differ from drawings that originate with a live model.

Use photographs if that's your thing, but use them sparingly. It may be hard to capture what you want to capture with a live model in front of you. You may believe that it is easier to draw from photographs because models breathe and slightly move at all times, even when in the same pose.

Keep working on it anyway. Doing so will reward you in spades as you progress.

A live model teaches you to observe, to see. In fact, you easily can hone your seeing by observing life. All art is about life and hardly restricted to a model.

When you draw, involve your senses. Then allow for the internal process and inner work to begin. This even includes shadow work; approaching areas that may feel uncomfortable for you. Stay with the process.

Know that as you practice and grow your artistic abilities and vision through focus, discipline, and concentration, you become a person who sees. This is no small matter, given that most of us have preconceived, mostly inaccurate notions of the forms in front of us and around us.

Drawing can be wild and messy, linear, free, expressive, and much more.

The intricacies of the human figure, its three-dimensional nature, its expressiveness and its ability to communicate emotions and attitudes make drawing the figure one of the most difficult endeavors. Learning to do so is an honor and a pleasure that requires effort and immense love for the form and its expression. It requires respect for the model besides deep self-reflection.

The great news is that the artist who can draw the human figure and do so well and with deep attention, can draw anything.

So let's get started.

*Learn the rules like a pro so you can break them
like an artist.—Pablo Picasso*

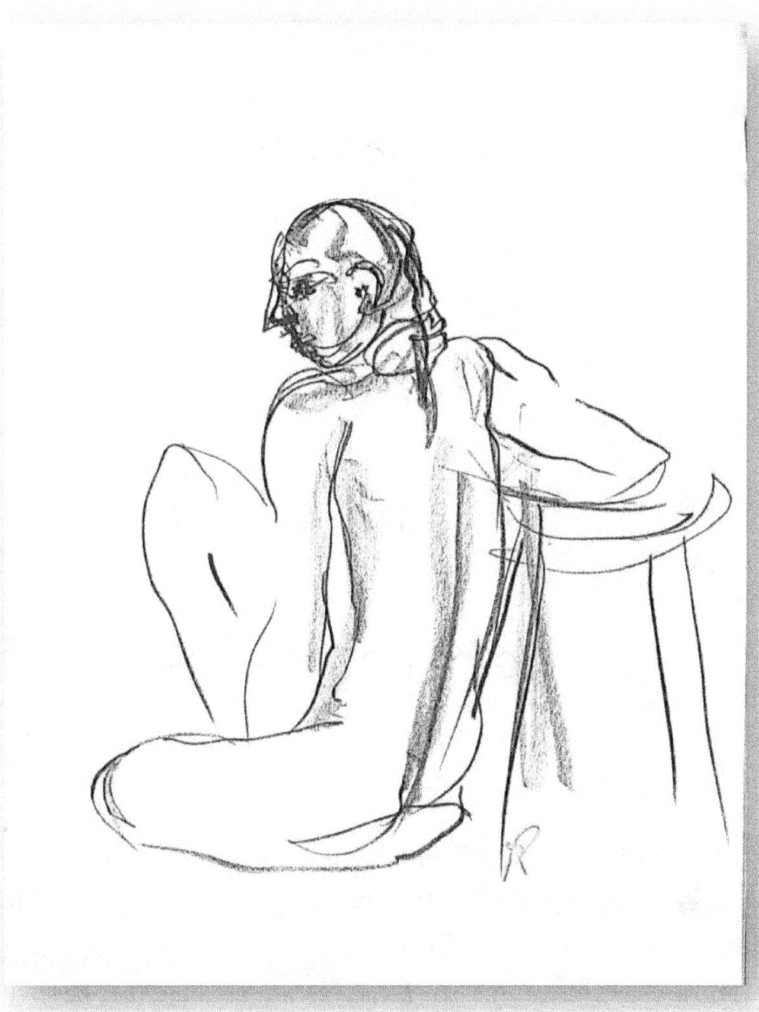

Figure 2 Inspired by Picasso and Matisse

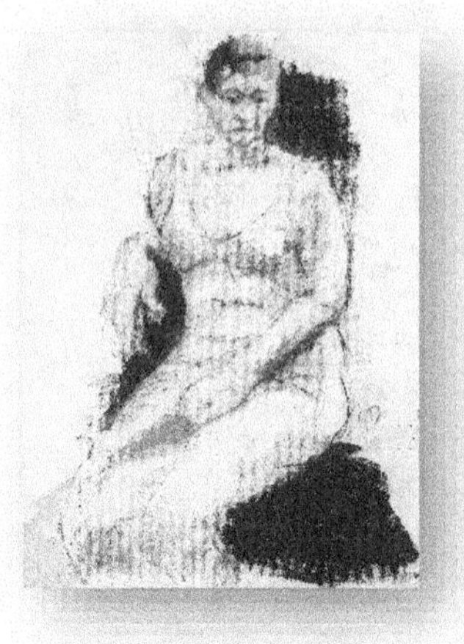

Chapter 1

How to Start a Drawing

Learning to See

Begin by quieting your mind so you can sense. Sensing is an invaluable component of seeing. As you do so, you'll see so much more, often seemingly small things and details that make all the difference-those a chattering mind is apt to miss. A quiet mind and originality are intimately linked.

Foremost, start your drawing out there, not on the paper. For me, that means walking around the model at a respectful distance and employing my arm, my hand, my fingers to air draw what I see. Doing this also often informs me of that which I have missed. Before I ever touch the paper, the beginning of the drawing imprints itself in my psyche.

By the way, drawing study options appear when a pose is in front of you by simply looking at the model from different positions.

I am drawing the model, something alive, and that must internalize into my drawing hand. What I call *air drawing* is a visceral way to create the drawing inside myself before it births itself on the paper.

Let the subject speak to you.

As mentioned in another book section, drawing a crude border into which to fit the figure on your paper helps you to stay on paper, unless you intentionally draw only a certain part of certain parts of the body. This border, which later you can either keep or integrate into the background, also shows what a curve is.

Always start at the feet, even if you cannot see them. In doing so, you will get a feeling for gesture. Read more about gesture in another section.

Starting with the feet, you acknowledge that the energy of the body springs up out of the floor. The center of the form's energy moves from place to place.

All forms need foundations. Otherwise, the drawing simply reflects a floating object. Let's start here: get a feeling for your paper and for the marks you make. Drive right through the pose.

But even though I just told you to start with the feet, in the first few seconds of the drawing indicate all parts of the body. Let your intuition guide you. When marks imply the entire body, you can, of course, start anywhere you wish. My suggestion is to start with a mark for the feet, then connect other parts. Work in broad strokes. Express the pose with economy, meaning with as few lines as possible.

The problem with details is that it is easy to get lost in them. So bring in the details last. You might find that they become almost superfluous.

Find the waist. Tilt the hips. Work toward transparent seeing by looking at negative shapes and at the overlap of the forms. I will return to this subject when discussing foreshortening.

Assess your paper and consider its edges a frame. You must stay within that frame. When I first drew, I struggled with staying on the paper, fitting the figure there. Although there are additional considerations for accomplishing this, such as proportion, light and shadow etc., for the moment let's just stay with the paper. It is a single sheet of paper or a sheet of paper that is part of a pad. In either case, I eventually tricked my mind into "seeing" the frame by drawing a crude but useful frame on the paper. These were close to the edges, and they immediately helped me in composing my drawings.

Using a viewer and measuring stick are also invaluable. The viewer helps the artist to compose the drawing and place the figure on the paper. The measuring stick assists with proportions and the relationships of the forms seen to each other. This same method clearly also applies to props, other materials, or backgrounds in the drawing.

When using the measuring stick, also consider the light source and find large blocks of value.

Here's how to work with the measuring stick, or either your pencil or charcoal standing in as measuring sticks.

Hold the measuring stick, pencil or charcoal between your thumb and fingers, then completely extend your arm and tilt your head towards the extended arm. That way, your eye aligns with the arm and its extension, the measuring stick. Mark off the measurement you are taking with the tip of the measuring stick and the first finger. Measure the model's head, then translate this measurement to the rest of the figure.

Transferring your measurement to your paper takes a bit of practice because the measurement is comparative. This means that you have to find the corresponding measurement(s) on your paper.

Some people have both eyes open when measuring, some close either the right or the left eye. This is personal preference. Experiment and see what works for you, always remembering to keep your arm extended and the eye or eyes as close as possible to the shoulder of that arm.

Correct measurements take time to learn. This is especially true because so many poses and perspectives exist. If you are looking at the figure from below or above, your measuring stick must find and assume the angle which corresponds to these views. The only time to hold the measuring stick perpendicular is at eye level. Practice, practice, practice. Eventually you will find you can accurately judge the angle at which to hold the measuring stick, pencil or charcoal.

Remember to keep your drawing flexible until it makes sense.

All elements this book discusses aim to help you, the artist, gain knowledge. Acquired knowledge creates a tapestry of invaluable resources, mostly unseen, but their knowledge invariably translates into your craft: drawing the human figure.

If you look, you'll get it. It's just that simple.—Sharon Pearson

---

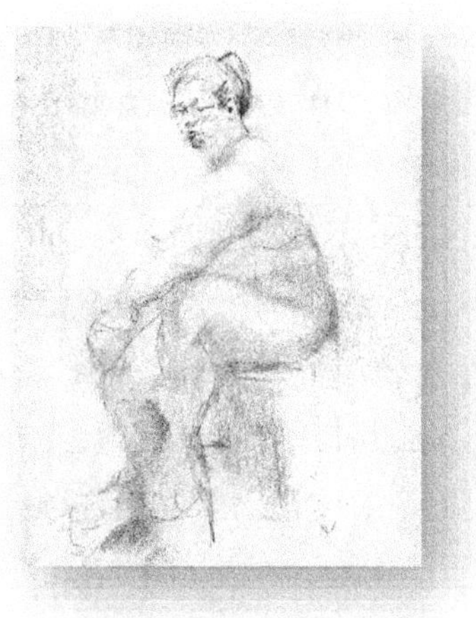

Chapter 2
Warm Up

Like an athlete about to go on a run or to play a game of tennis, warm up your body before you draw. Drawing is a physical activity just as much as it is a mental, emotional, and spiritual activity. Stretch before you move to your easel.

When you inhabit your body, it allows you to feel and absorb the model's poses and attitudes.

Observe the model. Walk around the model from ten or more feet away without disturbing other draftsmen and women. Do this to appreciate the three-dimensional form in front of you, to see how light and shadow affect the form, how foreshortening changes the form, how emotions transmit from the forms and poses. How different backgrounds, props, costumes etc. affect the ambiance and how the figure translates into one's visual field.

Do this also to assess the best possible set-up for your easel. More importantly, the initial few minutes you spend observing without so much as drawing one mark on your paper allows you to see more accurately, to understand the model's body in relationship to you, the observer and artist, to hone your focus, to find and even formulate your approach, and to relax into the intensity of what is in front of you.

Draw the figure as though it were transparent. Capturing its essence is almost as though there were nothing there.

The art that comes through you, translated from a three-dimensional form to a two-dimensional medium, originates from inside you. That can only happen if you internalize the form in front of you first; understood in its completeness versus focusing on minutiae. We'll return to this important point later in this manual.

Consider your goal, even your plan to stay connected to the drawing at all times, to render it in its totality, to capture its gesture over and over again.

Sculpt with your eyes.

Remember that the fundamentals free you. It is only that way the artist can become who he or she is, inclusive of style, verve, expression, and conviction.

There is immense value in starting your drawing sessions with quick poses. These poses may be 15 or 30 seconds long. They demand focus and concentration and notate only the essentials. Those may be a few simple gestural lines. They serve as studies of the subject, the model, and prepare you to capture what is in front of you.

Even longer or long poses benefit from spending 10 to 15 minutes drawing quick poses of the model first. In case you find yourself in a setting that does not offer them and jumps ahead to long poses, do them anyway. Then you can proceed into the longer pose from there.

Timed drawing of 1 minute, 3-minute, 5-minute, 10-minute, 20-minute, 30-minute, 40-minute, an hour-long or several hour poses all have value. And then there may be poses that last days. However, the longer the pose, the more challenging it is to keep it alive. That is another reason initial quick poses are so valuable.

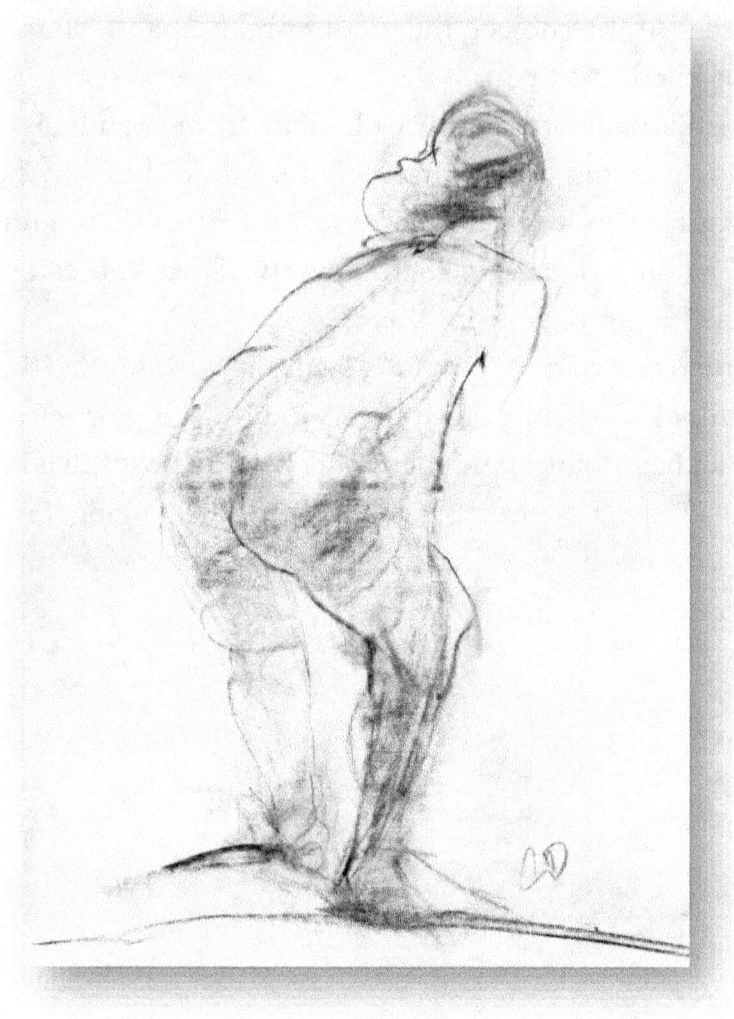

Figure 3 5-Minute Gesture Drawing

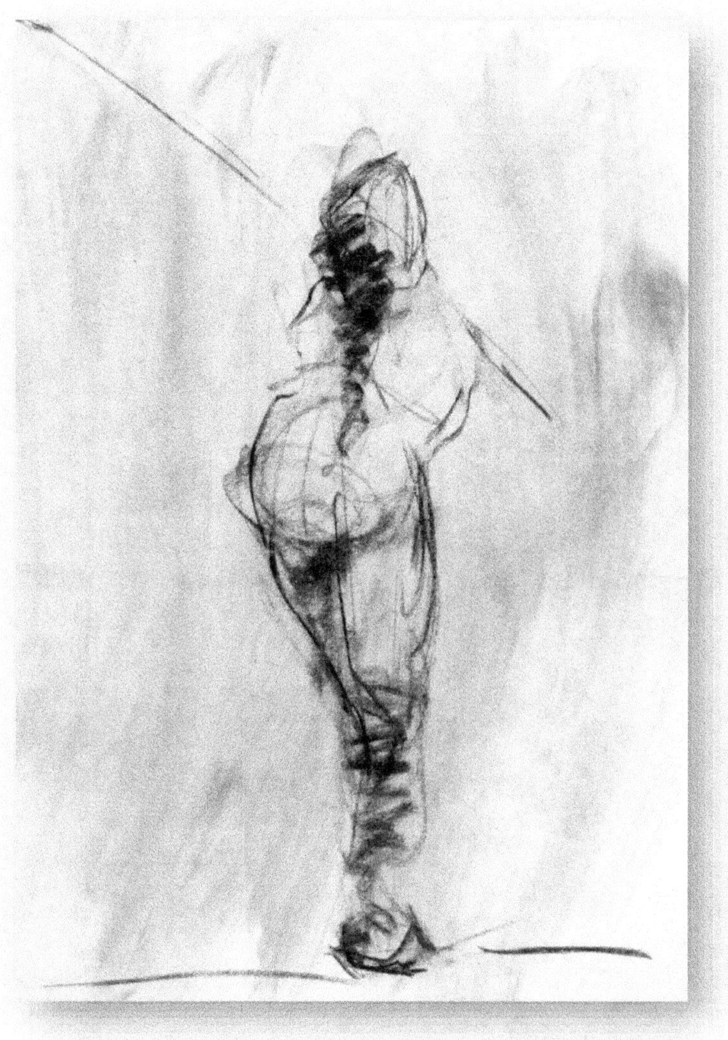

Figure 4 Another Gesture Drawing

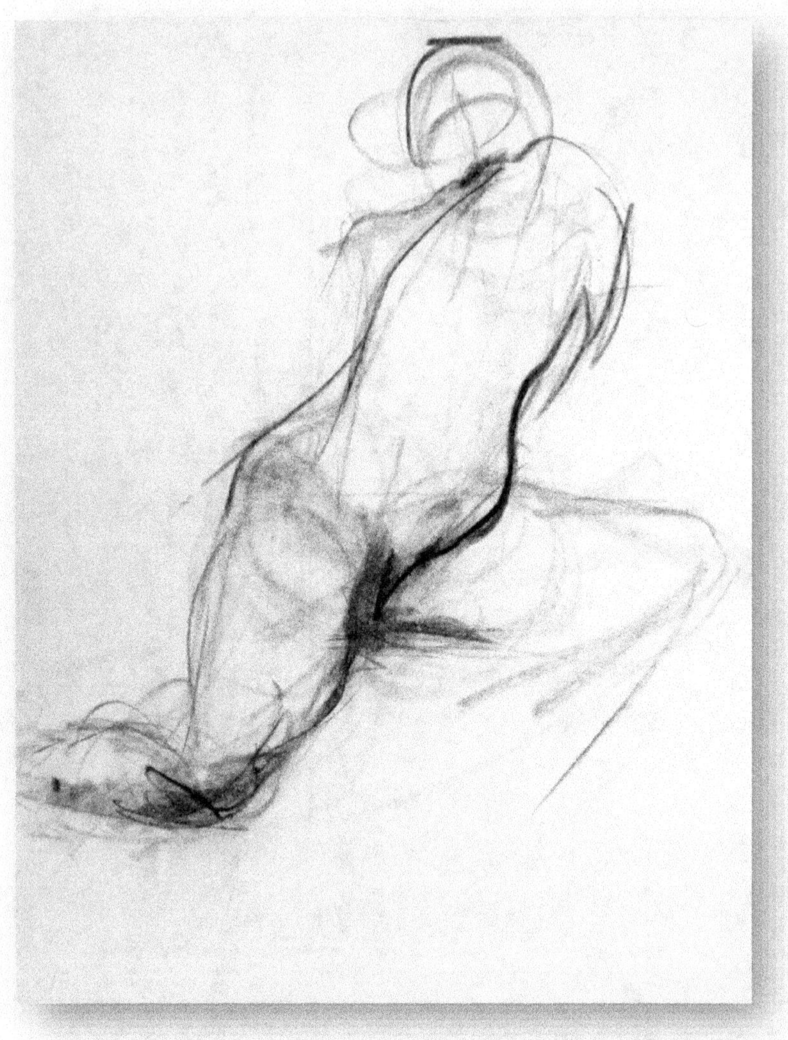

Figure 5 Gesture Drawing Capturing Foreshortening

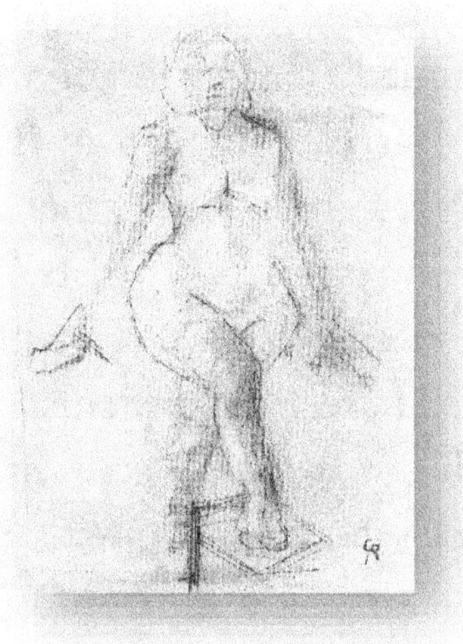

Chapter 3

Anatomy

Informing Your Drawings

One major pitfall of aspiring artists is drawing a figure's flesh, generally muscles, without consideration for the underlying bone structure of the skeleton. The results are strange looking figures that don't quite compute.

Although the figure appears in the artist's rendering, it looks off and it is not immediately apparent what the issue is. The way to fix this is to learn about anatomy and how it affects the appearance of the body and its movements.

Many books on anatomy for artists and artistic purposes exist. There is little need to rehash them here, but study them as often as you can. There are many surface things that happen on the body, which come from deep within it, and what you see will be much clearer when understanding anatomy. This study then needs expansion into muscle movements and tensions, how expression appears and which part of the body is most expressive. Kinesiology, the study of human movement that combines anatomy, biomechanics, physiology, and even neuropsychology, also offers important insights.

The internal structure of the body, anatomy for short, defines outward form. While the skeleton and its bones are mostly invisible to us, they provide the body's framework. The proportions of the body directly relate to anatomical structures. These also define the actions of the muscles, tendons, and ligaments. Muscles create surface forms held together by the underlying skeleton and organs and the figure's big envelope — the skin. You get the idea.

Study the spine and how it moves. Study the muscles[1] and know that when one muscle contracts its opposite and complementary muscle relaxes. Remember that muscles cross

---

[1] Myology is the study of muscles.

over joints, connected to them via tendons, to facilitate movement. They are the levers that move bones.

Hopefully, you find inspiration in your ability to develop inner or even X-ray vision by mastering anatomy. And no, there is no need to become a doctor or other medical professional. Artists only need a good understanding of anatomy as it relates to what they see and depict.

Incidentally, the artist who possesses this knowledge can draw correct figures from memory. So, as you build your anatomical arsenal, regularly test yourself by drawing the body from memory.

My own anatomical learning continues. I find it helpful to review anatomical drawings and texts on a regular basis. Instead of "dry" learning, the smaller anatomical models art stores sell come in handy here. But over the years I have taken anatomy courses and drawn in medical school cadaver dissection labs, though the pungent formaldehyde fumes in them only allowed for short exposures.

I return to Michaelangelo once more. He studies human anatomy in depth and detail. He feverishly, passionately, and untiringly sketched bones, muscles, and sinews. Overwhelmingly, these sketches originated from his visits to morgues where he dissected cadavers by candlelight.

This idea may not appeal to you and may even be difficult to pursue. You can still become quite adept at anatomy as it relates to artistic endeavors. You might do so via the exercises at the end of this section, via instruction from a qualified teacher, via enrolling in a community college anatomy course, and so on.

One last comment about anatomy for artists is that your power of observation amplifies with its study, but anatomy contributes mechanical artistic knowledge. It leads to more fluid expression of one's craft, yet is only one part of the artist's work.

Structure lends the figure integrity. This is just as true in drawing the figure. Without structure, the figure and the drawing fall apart and become piecemeal.

Think of anatomy as the scaffolding in drawing the figure. It works in tandem with understanding of the figure's forms in their abstract geometrical shapes, which lends a 3D sense to the drawing.

However, a structural drawing of the figure will look stiff and lifeless without capturing the gesture of the figure, first the overall gesture of the pose, then the gestures of the forms that make up the figure. More about gesture later, though.

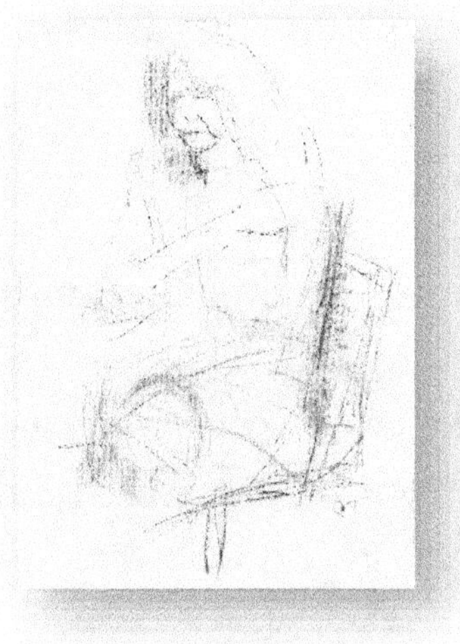

Chapter 4

Masses and Centers

Simplifying the Human Form

Isolation of the major body masses is more important than focusing on details like eyelashes, fingernails and the like. Each mass has a center, yet all masses connect. The spine unites the different parts of the body, while limiting the movements of the head, chest and pelvis. Distribution of the masses allows for balance and symmetry.

Resist the temptation to draw details because getting lost in those disintegrates drawings. The detail often has no relation to the structure it belongs to and disconnects from the mass to which it belongs.

The head, the shoulders, the chest, the torso, the arms, the hands, the hips, the legs, the feet are masses. Of these forms, the torso is the biggest and most important one. Find the center of the torso. One easy way to do so is to take your measuring stick and measure from the base of the throat on down. The waist is the narrowest part of the torso. Make sure you know where it is.

All masses relate to the ground from which they arise. Imagine the body coming out of the ground. Visualize the effects of gravity on the body.

Know that weightless bodies exist only in space without the effects of gravity. So let the body you draw adhere to gravitational law. Otherwise, it will simply float on your paper.

The human body comprises three movable masses: the head, the rib cage, and the pelvis. Think of the masses as levers in which muscles, tendons and ligaments move. Muscles work in tandem, meaning one muscle pulls against another. The muscle that pulls is taut, its complement inert.

Find the masses and their centers. Build on them. When you see two forms, aim to know how they relate. Then identify the line of gravity with your measuring stick.

When viewing the body from the front, find the pit of the neck and from there the plumb line to the feet. See where that line goes. —When viewing the body from the back, draw a vertical line from the neck to the feet. See how this line relates to the angles the pose presents.

Basic geometric forms and volumes underlie all forms. For you, that means focusing on these underlying forms versus on surface appearances. In doing so, you model the form and marry structure and design.

For example, the neck is a cylindrical shape that moves up and down and from side to side. It also rotates. The occipital bone and the neck connect at the atlas, the first cervical vertebra. It comprises seven cervical vertebrae.

When you uncover the body's essential masses and its inner forms, the underlying mechanisms of the body become more transparent.

Treat nature by the cylinder, sphere, cone…

—Paul Cezanne

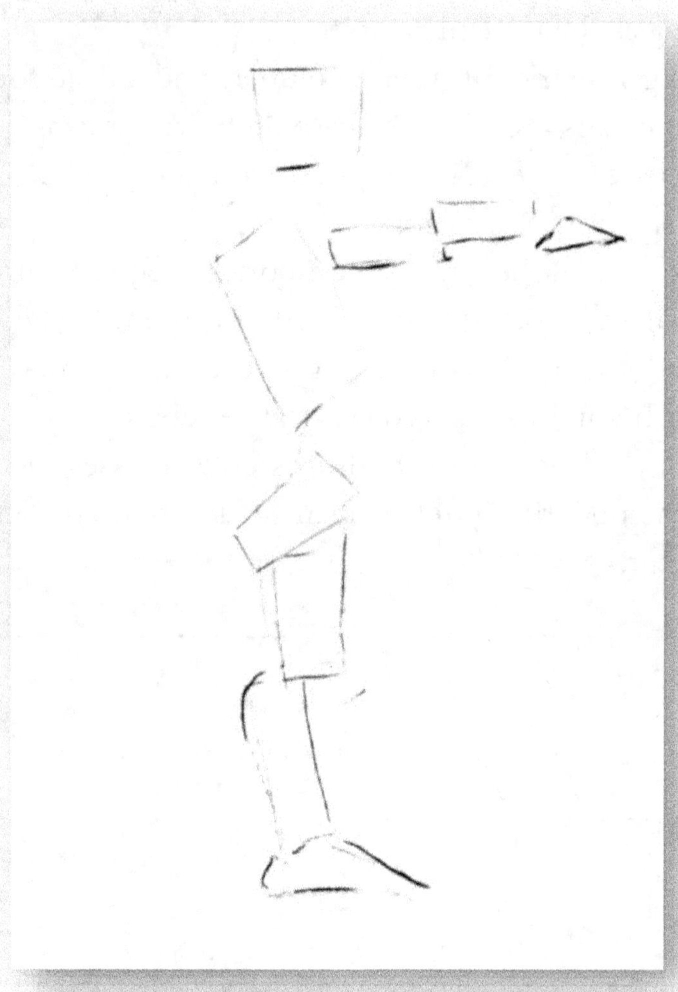

Figure 6 Abstracted Forms and Masses

Drawing is like life. You've got to start in the center of things in order to *get it.*

Look for the overall or broad view and work from large to small. Develop X-ray vision and look into the form and into the pose. What you, the artist, see and draw directly communicates to what viewers see.

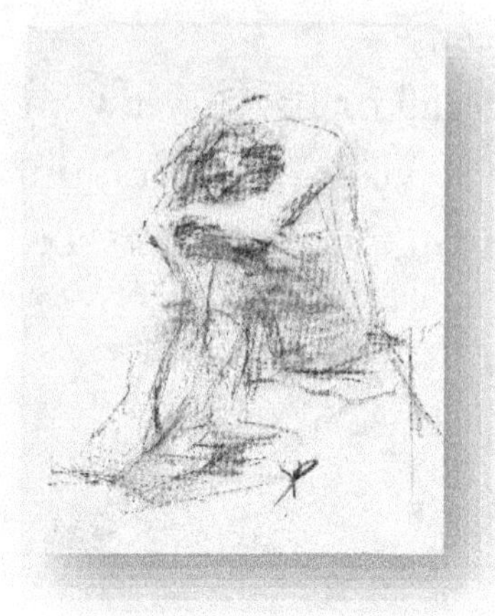

Chapter 5

Volume and Weight

Modeling the Human Form

When drawing the figure, the artist's skill in communicating the three-dimensional nature of the human form on a two-dimensional medium quickly becomes apparent. But how to give the gestures and lines on the paper a three-dimensional appearance?

The aim is to show the body's fullness, weight, and roundness. Volume lends the figure weight and shows gravitational pull. It also emphasizes the visual weight in a work of art.

To achieve volume, review how shapes that have depth to them work. Review the sections on masses and centers and on weight. They are great starting points and directly relate to creating volume on the paper.

When working with masses and centers abstract them into geometrical forms, like a cube or a box or a sphere. Then shade these forms to create depth and differentiation.

As you progress, add hatching and cross-hatching to define the form further and give it even more depth and differentiation. Hatching and cross-hatching refer to parallel and intersecting lines. These lines can be quite fine or coarser, depending on you and your approach. The closer together your hatch and cross-hatch lines, the darker that area of your drawing. With their you, you become the sculptor of the human form on paper. Eventually, you may also find that this work interests you so much that you explore sculpting in clay or metal or another medium.

For now, we're staying with drawing the figure, though.

Once you master masses and centers, shading, and hatching and cross-hatching, employ perspective in a new way. What I mean here is to pay attention and see that even though you are drawing the model, meaning one person, some parts of that model are closer to the viewer, you.

Parts closer to you will be higher in contrast, in detail, and in definition. Parts farther away are less defined and softer. Train your eye to see these differences.

Next, pay attention to shadow areas because light reflects, and that creates subtle differences in shadow areas. Shadow areas, therefore, have highlights in them, something for you to perceive and incorporate into your drawing. Render these highlights subtly or your shadows will look strange.

Perhaps the most challenging way to give volume to the figure is through foreshortening. In a foreshortened pose, certain forms of the figure either recede in space or come closer. Because there is a balance in the body, the forms which come forward and those which recede work in tandem. This is true even when you cannot see both forms.

Foreshortening is challenging for any artist. Master it, however much study and practice it takes for you. When you succeed in this, your figures come alive.

Weight and balance align. When observing a standing figure, its center-of-gravity starts at the pit of the neck and extends to or passes through the supporting foot or feet. In a pose where both feet support the weight equally, the center of gravity passes between the feet. The body's proportions inform its weight and center of gravity. For females, that center is above the pubic bone. For males, it is at the pubic bone.

The center of gravity in children shifts from sitting at the navel at birth to shifting to the level of the iliac bone at age three, etc.

More fat pads female hips besides the proportional differences.

When a figure stands straight, it does not move and is static. Any bending, turning or twisting changes the figure's center of gravity and with it its balance. This also relates to foreshortening.

Notice where the weight appears in a standing pose. Unless the model stands in a frontal, completely aligned, and static position in front of you, the weight is likely to be on one leg.

You can test this out by doing a quick assessment when standing by bending or turning to one side. Which leg carries the weight to support your body in these positions?

When you draw the model, see how he or she carries the body's weight. Simple initial shading, being darker in weight-bearing limbs, shows the weight.

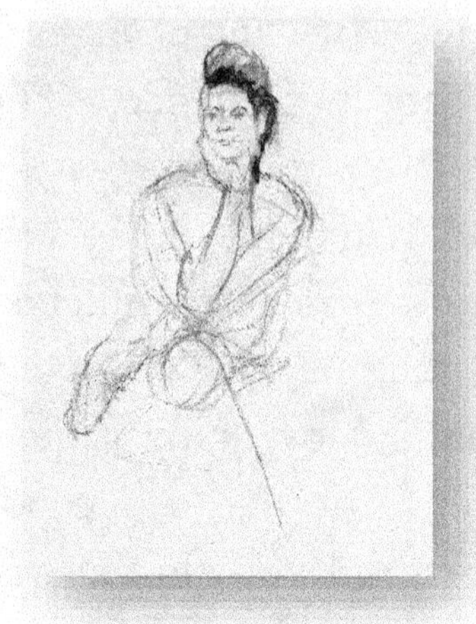

Chapter 6

Composition

Balancing a Drawing and its Design

C omposition matters. It helps you place the figure right. In doing so, you work with negative space, something I discuss a little later.

Good composition creates a sense of balance. It is therefore important to compose your drawing and never to forget the shape of your format (paper).

Subdivision, visual weight, tension all play roles. These and accurate measurements provide the artwork with balance, expression, and confidence.

This relates to good design, and such design guides the viewer. It drives how the viewer perceives the drawing. A drawing's focal point draws the eye and sends a message.

Great compositions balance the weight and visual elements in a drawing and lend meaning to the drawing by displaying harmonies, dissonances, and tensions, etc. In figure drawing, anatomical knowledge aids in the design and composition of your drawing.

Such compositions are easily available for view and study in museums and art books.

To delve deeper into composition, read Rudolf Arnheim's excellent book The Power of the Center. This is a classic on composition and provides an art historical journey to boot. Other books on composition exist, but few go to the depth of this book.

All great composition starts with a view towards the bigger picture with an intimate understanding of what the viewer sees. Such compositions place the figure on the page where it looks natural and interesting. Always remember that when starting with one leg, you are approaching the whole figure.

Play with different paper formats to find out which format allows for the best composition for your purposes. Drawing an imaginary frame onto the paper also helps in staying on the paper versus running off it. It looks quite awkward, for example, when feet or heads are cut off because the composition and likely the figure's proportions either were never considered or were incorrect.

Your decision to use your paper horizontally or vertically is an important component of your composition. Next, consider dividing your paper into three equal segments from top to bottom and from left to right. Doing so helps you decide where the focal points of your drawing ought to be. These usually are where the lines you lightly draw on your paper intersect. Although you will have four such focal points to choose from, most viewers naturally gravitate to those on the right. But the decision of how to direct the viewer's experience when looking at your drawing is yours.

A little compositional planning is advantageous because it can save you frustration later. However, if you keep your drawing flexible as advocated elsewhere in this volume, you might well be able to shift your composition, meaning the placement of the figure on the page. Still, your initial attention to the correct placement of the figure serves you well.

The lines to help you divide the paper are aids that may be useful to you when first learning about composition. Many artists, including myself, rely on their intuition about where to place the drawing object or objects. Soon you'll do the same.

Another great tool is a viewer, which you can make out of a piece of cardboard. It functions similar to the way a camera works; as you look through it, placing the figure in a balanced compositional way becomes second nature.

Composition associates all parts of a work of art: the figure and its placement in its environment. Doing so imbues meaning into your drawings. Line, value, light and shade, shape, space, volume, and even texture[2] all contribute to good design in a work of art. However, this is true only when these elements visually balance.

The composition is the organized sum of the interior functions of every part of the work.—Wassily Kandinsky

---

---

[2] Texture creates the tactile feeling of materials like silk, wool and hair.

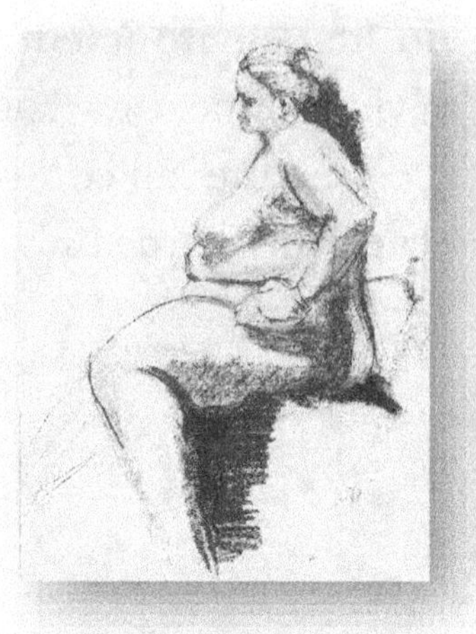

Chapter 7

Negative space

The Spaces around and in-between the Figure

Composition and negative space closely intertwine. Using negative space makes or breaks a composition. But what is negative space?

Simply put, it is the space between a drawing's subject, in this case the figure, and the rest of the page or image. The figure also has negative spaces between limbs, for example. Negative space is air space. Yet, even though it is empty space, it shapes the drawing's subject and designs how the viewer reads it.

Negative space simplifies and focuses on the essential. It exists in all art forms, including in sculpture, photography, graphic design, and music.

The ability to simplify means to eliminate the unnecessary so that the necessary may speak.— Hans Hofmann

---

By placing a figure a certain way on the page, you create negative space and with it in total a composition. Some effects of negative space, when mastered, are:

- A balanced composition
- Creation of a unique perspective
- Lending the drawing depth and dimension
- A more accurate representation of the figure
- Imbuing a drawing with symbolism

Negative space is important for all these reasons. To comprehend it and its varied uses, study artists' compositions throughout time. If you love modern art, look at Picasso,

Matisse, Van Gogh and others. See how they used it and what effects they created.

The book on composition I mentioned in the previous section also explains its use and effects, and shows great examples.

Negative space equates to embracing the void, the empty space, the unseen. It takes time to see in this new way and to practice it.

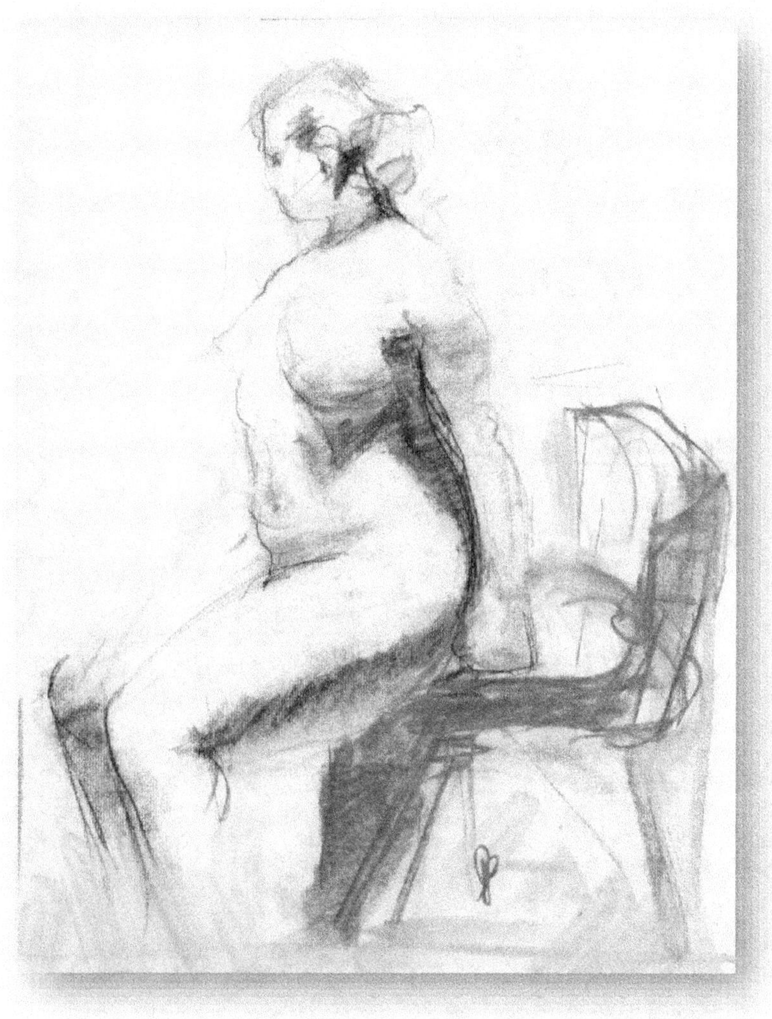

Figure 7 Negative Space Inside and Outside the Figure

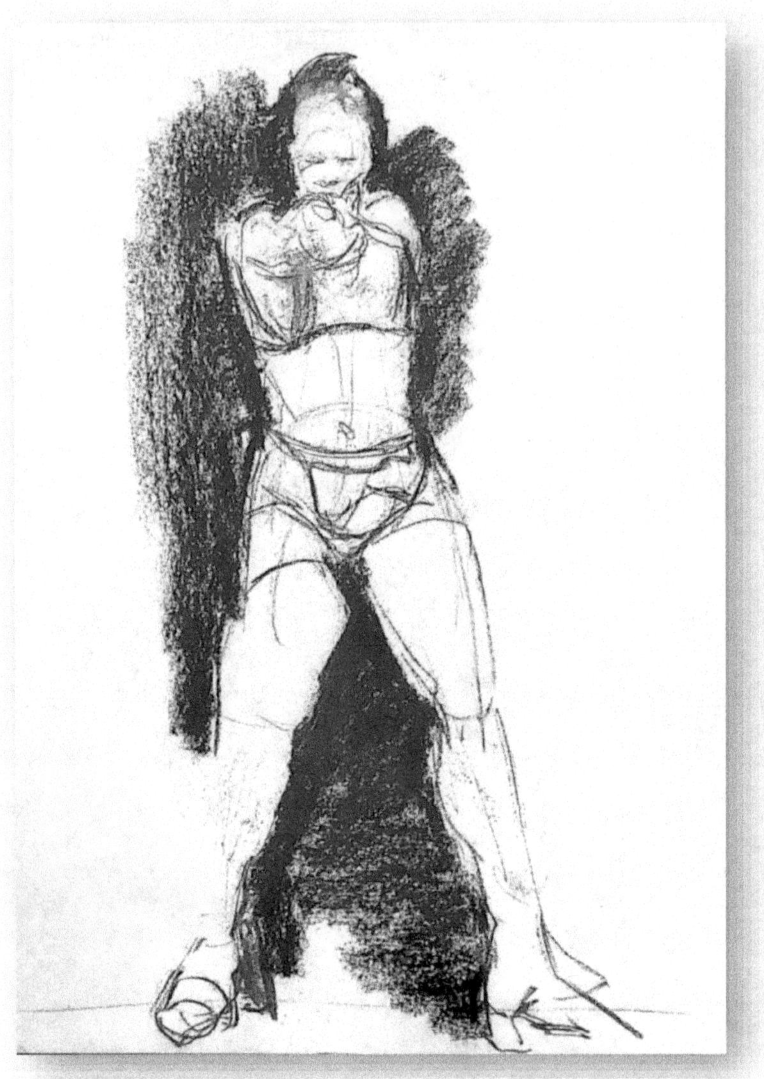

Figure 8 The Spaces in between the Figure

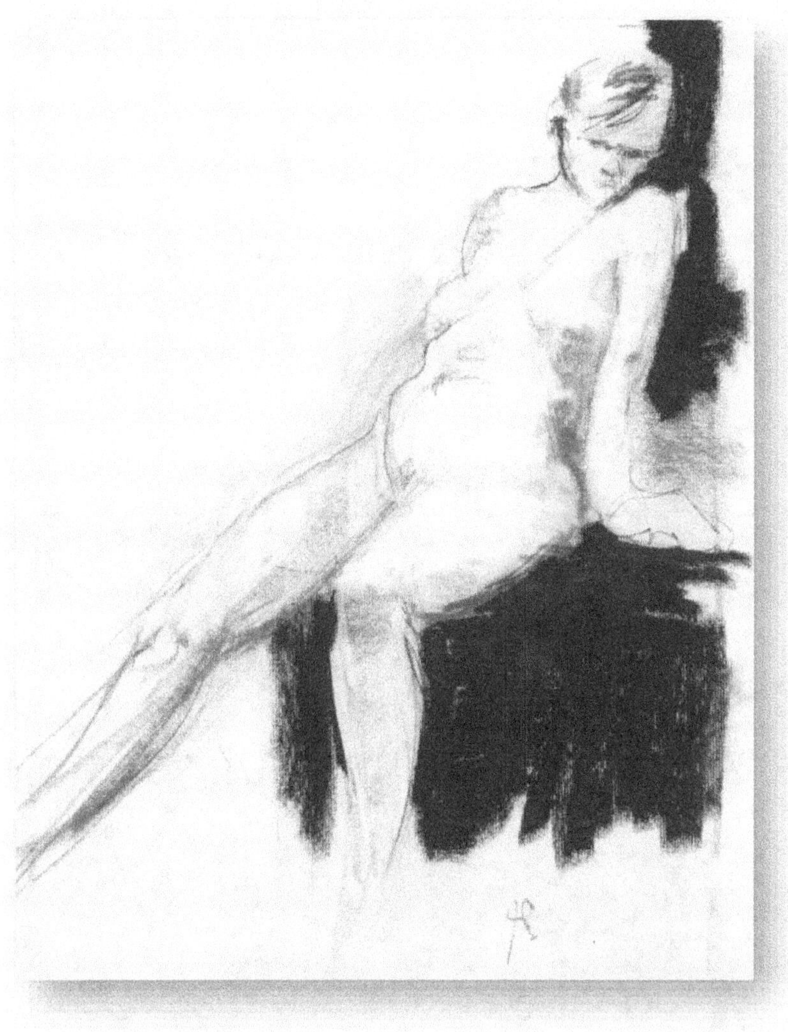

Figure 9 Negative Space Surrounding the Figure

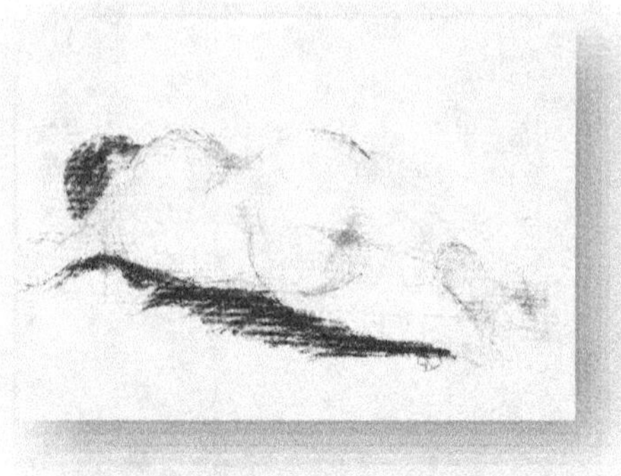

Chapter 8

Perspective

Allowing for three-dimensions

Although perspective[3] is an exceedingly important topic for drawing anything, including the human figure, delving into exceeds the parameters of this book. The best way to gain a deep understanding of perspective

---

[3] The Latin verb perspicere which means to see across is the root of the word perspective.

and its importance in drawing is to enroll in a basic drawing class.

You may also study books specific to this subject and study draftsmen and -women throughout time.

Perspective affects a drawing's focal point, meaning where and how the eye travels. All perspective rests on the fact that objects that recede in space appear smaller. It refers to how objects and planes appear at a distance. It relates to the center of vision where retreating lines come toward the level of the eye and meet at a point. Various perspectives exist and their vanishing points meet at different places. Learning about it is a basic drawing prerequisite.

If the artist does not understand perspective and how to see and use it, all the applications of paint and ink and pencil will not overcome the lack of good perspective.—Helen Scott

---

The laws of perspective refer to both the artist's and the viewer's line of sight. Although it is possible for a drawing to contain several focal points, e.g. perspectives, this topic is beyond the scope of this book.

The farther away the figure is, the smaller it appears. The same is true for any parts of the body, so if your model leans back, the parts that lean away from you are smaller and the parts closer to you are larger.

You now also understand the role of perspective plays in foreshortened forms a little better.

Some descriptions of various perspective techniques follow. Yes, these are invented constructs in art, whether in drawing or architecture. Knowing which ones exist and to what purpose will help you in drawing. Here, then, are the different perspectives in use.

In parallel or linear perspective[4] lines appear to converge at a point in the distance as they travel back in space. They are, in effect, traveling away from the viewer. Again, objects in the distance appear smaller. This illusion to depict spatial depth in a two-dimensional medium creates a view in which everything in the drawing moves toward a single vanishing point. A famous example of this is Leonardo da Vinci's The Last Supper.

In an angular or oblique perspective, there are two vanishing points. Yes, even perspective has complexity. It is possible to combine various perspective techniques, but that is once mastering the basics is in place. Linear perspective allows for accurate depiction of objects, including the figure, in space.

Atmospheric or aerial perspective refers to atmospheric effects that happen when something is viewed from a distance. Let's say you're on top of a hill looking at a town below you. In that scenario, the features in the distance blur and appear hazy. Tonal contrasts fade, as do colors. Famous examples of aerial

---

[4] This is a brief description of parallel or linear perspective in its simplest form only.

perspective include Leonardo's Mona Lisa and Richard Diebenkorn's Berkeley Series. As you study these paintings, you will see how aerial perspective transmits the three-dimensionality of space and the air that fills it.

For learning to draw the figure and to improve your drawing ability, remember that the laws of perspective apply to drawing the figure. Since this book only covers this topic in rudimentary terms, please seek a class that introduces basic drawing skills, read books on the topic, and visit museums to study the subject via the drawings and paintings in them. The Dutch artist M. C. Escher (1898-1972) was a master of perspective, to the point of influencing how you and other viewers see and perceive artworks today.

One thing you'll grasp is that perspective and foreshortening are on intimate terms. For example, when looking at one plane of a cube, the other two planes of the cube are foreshortened. This means they are shorter than the plane you're looking at. If that makes little sense to you as yet, it will when reading the rest of the book.

For now, just know that depending on your line of sight—at eye level with the model, from below or from above the model, etc. —you see one form and the others turned away at the same time. Even a standing front view pose contains foreshortening, however slight.

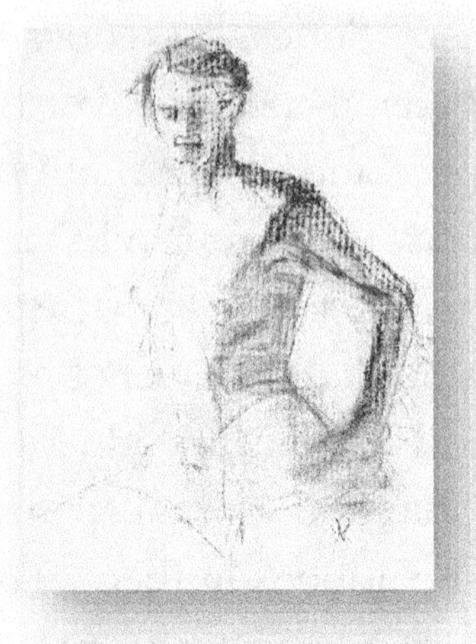

Chapter 9

Planes

Creating Dimensions on Flat Surfaces

When looking at the body, note the planes you see. Planes refer to flat surface, and they inform geometric shapes that help delineate them. They are important in structure, weight, composition, modeling the figure, and more. When modeling the forms of the figure, your ability to identify planes is crucial.

Planes are a big subject and one every artist eventually must master. In basic drawing classes, students spend considerable time modeling geometric shapes which teach them about planes and their relationship to any form they draw, whether a still life, a landscape or the human figure.

Structure may be understood via planes, which are flat or curved surfaces. These also show any object's position in space.

Learning about them, modeling them, and shading them helps the artist to deal with light and shadow. It also informs the three-dimensionality of objects. The human figure contains these forms and masters like Picasso and Matisse abstracted, abbreviated, and simplified their work through them, while the human figure or any other object they drew remained fully recognizable.

You can do the same, though I recommend that for now, especially as a beginner, you use them to render the figure in classical terms. Picasso was an exquisite draftsman whose rigorous classical training produced stunning and beautiful classic figure drawings long before his famous figurative abstractions.

The correct outlining of the body's planes afford the correct shading of the body's forms. Put in shadows first in your drawing, after correctly drawing the body's planes, then develop your value scales, and gradually put the values in your drawing, always double checking those against the shadows.

Shadow planes that are nearest to a light source will appear darker than other areas of the same shadow. This is also known as the law of contrasts.[5]

Planes inform perspective and what the eye sees, creating a palpable and immediate connection to the manner in which to place and compose a drawing.

Through the planes, artists can effectively compose, bringing their point of view, or for lack of a better term, their message into focus.

Composing a drawing of the head or hand or the entire figure from either the front, the side or the top, for example, provides different perspectives and visual effects.

You can abstract the entire human body as planes, whether head, feet, hands, torso, or legs. That makes your work easier once you understand and appreciate planes, and much harder to impossible if lacking.

---

[5] Michel Eugène Chevreul, The Principles of Harmony and Contrast of Colour and Their Applications to the Arts.

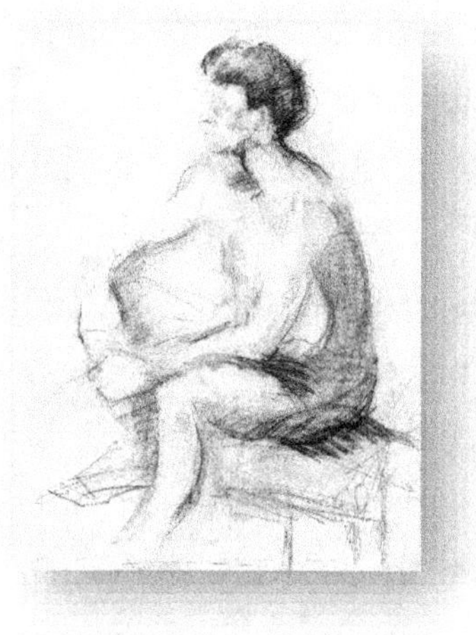

Chapter 10

Proportions

Relating the body's parts

Proportions hold your drawings together and give them a solid foundation. Just as a house would fall apart with a poor or improper foundation underneath it, so do drawings. Proper proportions lend your figure the support it needs. They also provide you with visual references.

A human body is a structural and mechanical marvel. Proportions are its foundation, its scaffolding. Just as a house can dangerously lean and thus induce an impending collapse, artistic execution and vision collapse without proper proportions. If an enormous head sits on a tiny body, the immediate effect is imbalance. The result is an odd overall appearance, which also affects a drawing's composition, realism and emotional power.

While there are artists, such as cartoonists, who draw figures out of proportion, purposefully so, that is an entirely different subject. If you want to excel at drawing the human figure, practice drawing correct proportions. Use imaginary lines to assess proportion. Those are the lines already discussed elsewhere in this text.

It is a common mistake to draw the figure to get the proportions wrong. I perpetrated that mistake and it took time and attention to correct it. When I first drew, learning about the body's proportions was a challenge. Over time and with constant practice, things shifted for the better.

Simply put, proportion is about the relationship of one thing to another.

For the human body, the standard measurement for it is the head[6]. Translated this means measuring—with your measuring stick—first the model's head from the top of the skull to the

---

[6] Note that the size of the hand generally equates one head.

chin, then with that measure demarcated with your finger or fingernail on the stick, assessing the other measurements. How many heads make up the length of the body from the top of the skull to the feet? How many the clavicles and shoulders, the rib cage, the pelvic area, the hands and feet and so on?

The overall for a figure standing tall with no bending or twisting involved is approximately seven and a half heads. Even the tallest person is no larger than eight heads. The seven and half heads proportion measurements deviate, depending on gender, age and race. Every person also has individual differences, even if they are ever so slight.

Proportional differences exist in males, females, and children.

For males, the greatest width is just below the shoulders at the deltoids. That width is some two heads. Male hips measure about one and a half heads. The male neck and trunk make up some two and three-quarter heads, and the lower extremities (the hips and legs) measure approximately three and three-quarter heads. The lower arms from the fingertips to the elbows measure two heads.

For females, several important anatomical variations exist. They include female bones being shorter than the male's. The female pelvis is broader and shallower, lending more width to the hips. The female's sacrum is wider than the males and it sits at a different angle, which goes backward. That difference in the female pelvis lengthens the distance between the rib cage and the pelvis.

Female shoulders are narrower than the male's, and female collar bones and arms are shorter. The legs of the female may be long or short while the female torso generally is longer than the male's. These variations make it difficult to judge the height of the female's body when she sits.

These differences in the sexes project different appearances. For instance, male shoulders show more squarely than their more graceful female counterparts. And male hips are narrower than female hips.

And here is what you need to know when drawing children. Children's bodies change over time as they transition from infancy, through childhood, and adolescence to adulthood. That means a baby has different proportions than a child of two or three, than a child of ten, than an adolescent in puberty, than a young adult. The variations are considerable and they continue until approximately the age of twenty-five when the body is full grown. Over time, the relative sizes of the head and the trunk change. For this reason, it is impractical to give proportional measurements for children.

As the body ages, its proportions shift yet again. The body adds more fat while bones shrink, cartilage becomes less pliable, and muscles lose strength and flexibility. Between ages 25 and 90, the body begins to change. At 25 years of age, you may recall, the body is fully grown. Its decline begins then, but its effects usually take two or more decades to become noticeable.

Overall, the aging body changes in height and resiliency. That is true for all body systems, whether they be organs, bones, muscles, joints, skin, or hair. A more compact upper body with leaner legs. Knowing and keenly observing this helps you as an artist.

Once again, in paying attention to these, you hone your powers of observation with accuracy. Measuring improves accuracy. It is essential to understand the figure and in representing it realistically.

This entire section details proportions as they apply to a figure that stands erect. When the figure twists, turns, bends, and moves, certain forms shorten or lengthen. This foreshortening means a shift in proportional perspective, even though the underlying human anatomy clearly does not change.

As a side note, when you study the masters you may see ideal proportions that stylize the figure. But the proportions given in this section refer to those applicable to drawing a human figure correctly.

At this point, I want to point out that measuring with your measuring stick is indispensable. Measuring, though, starts before ever picking up the measuring stick via your eyes. That means you study the model with your eyes first. As you move on your artistic journey, you will find that measuring with your eyes becomes second nature and takes little time.

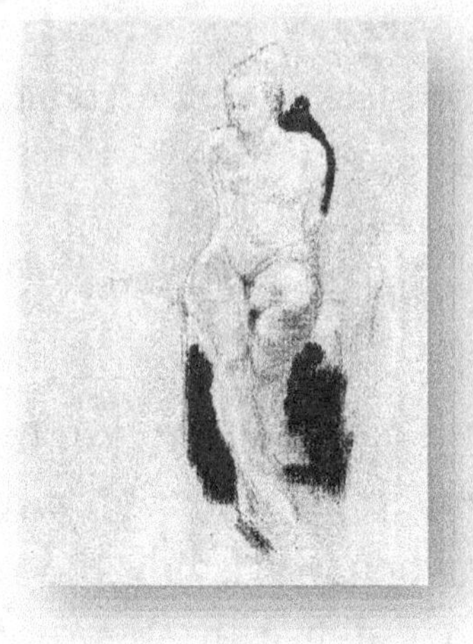

Chapter 11

Foreshortening

Projecting or Receding Forms

Foreshortening is challenging for any artist. Master it, however much study and practice it takes for you. When you succeed in this, your figures come alive. Foreshortening happens when viewing the body and the pose from different angles. Forms begin to overlap and sometimes completely overlap. Forms come forward in space or recede in space. This creates visual distortion of forms.

Think of foreshortening as the skeleton in action. The greater the degree of foreshortening, the more a plane's width reduces. What you are seeing in a foreshortened pose is an actual shortening of one or more of the body's planes.

Foreshortening is a technique that coalesces with perspective. Your understanding of how forms shift because of different perspectives informs what you see. And even though there will be forms that belong to the human figure that cannot be seen in various perspectives, you must know what they are because they still need to connect to what you actually see and draw. Foreshortening then, rendered effectively, creates the illusion of depth in a drawing.

The human body is a complex form and difficult to draw from any angle.

Angles that are particularly difficult to draw happen when viewing the figure from above or below. Similarly, when a figure turns, twists, or bends, foreshortening appears in its forms. As you read the last few sentences, it probably occurs to you that foreshortening, or a change in perspective, happens in almost all poses.

Still, foreshortening is most pronounced in the extreme viewpoints that occur when poses have pronounced qualities of bending, twisting, and so on. This is also true for poses viewed from above or below.

In order to understand how distortions appear, study forms like rectangles, squares, ellipses, and so on.

When forms are distorted, the viewer sees only certain things. However, the other unseen forms depend on knowledge of the structure of the thing, in this case the figure. Yes, I know, this is yet another return to structure, anatomy and rhythm.

Use both gravity and angles as quick sketching aids by putting your measuring stick to work. Put in imaginary lines to relate the angles you see to one another when drawing the figure.

Find the waist. The waist is an ellipse. Tilt the hips. Work toward transparent seeing by looking at negative shapes and at the overlap of the forms.

Most beginning figure drawing artists experience difficulties when severe foreshortening is present. It presents challenges that include the beginner's knowledge of what an arm or leg or any other form looks like. While many beginners see the foreshortening of a leg, for example, they rely on what a leg is supposed to look like versus the form actually there.

Yet, most beginners can accurately draw the foreshortening of geometric forms. That is good news because as the section on Masses and Centers discusses, abstracting the figure into geometric shapes is a wonderful way to understand and capture the human body well. To reiterate, the shape of a form defines its position in space and conveys important clues about its structure. A form comprises various planes, some of which are completely foreshortened and which equate to the edges of the form.

The ability to comprehend a form's shape as if it were a flat puzzle-piece is an essential perceptual skill.—Nathan Goldstein

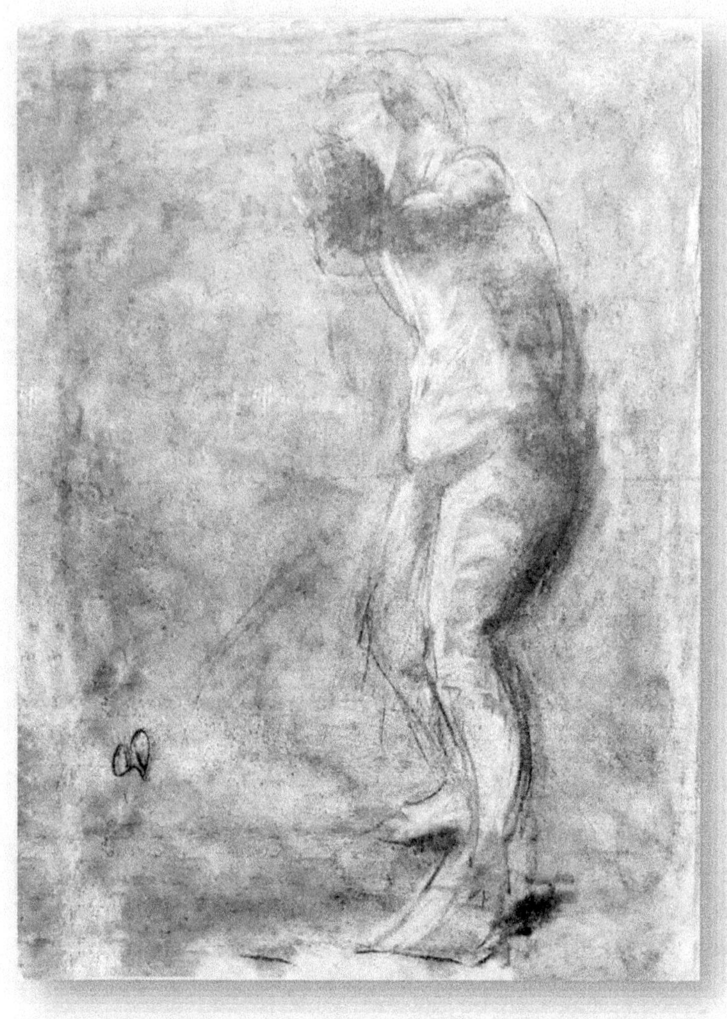

Figure 10 Foreshortened Male Figure

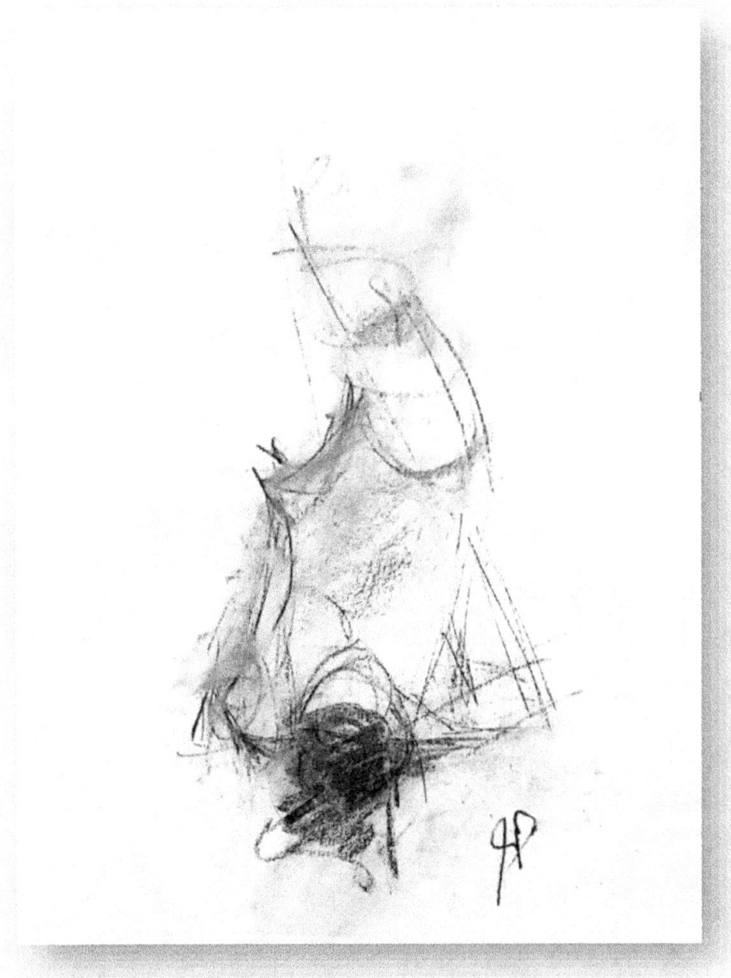

Figure 11 Foreshortened Female Figure

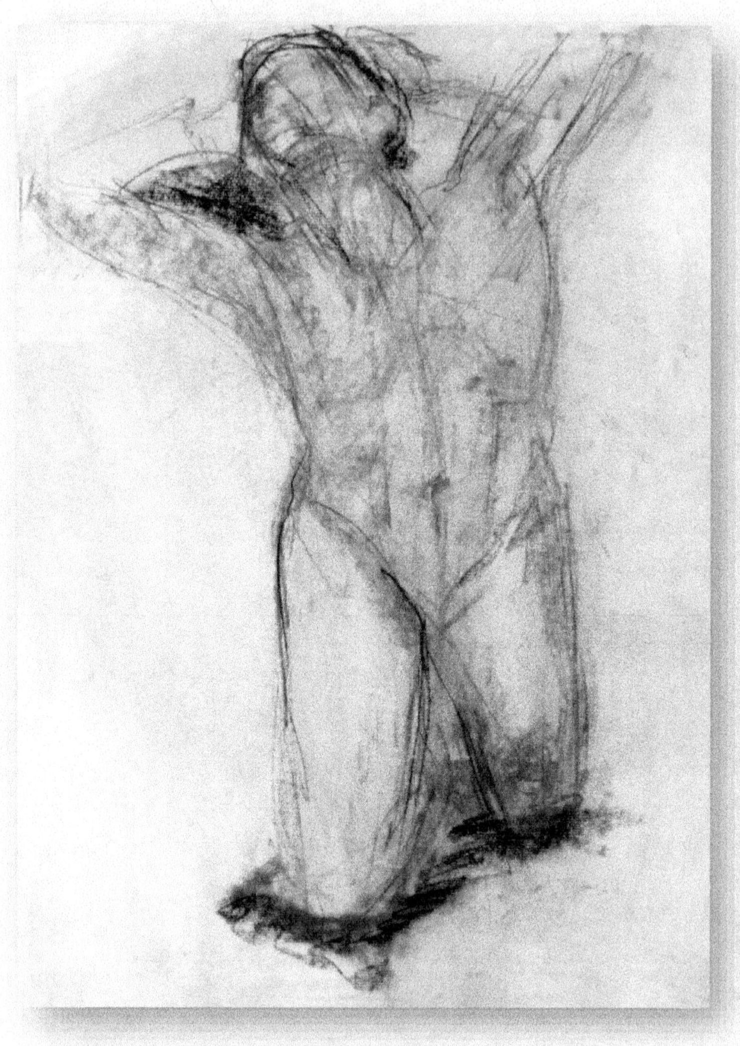

Figure 12 Foreshortened Figure

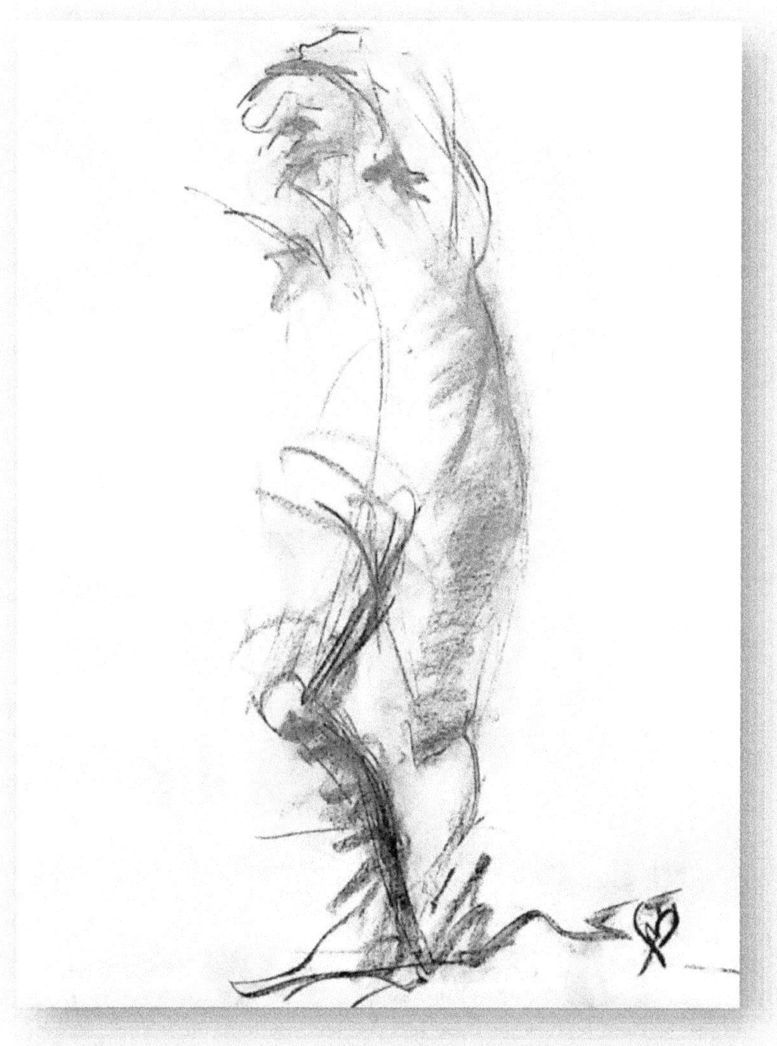

Figure 13 Twisting and Bending Figure

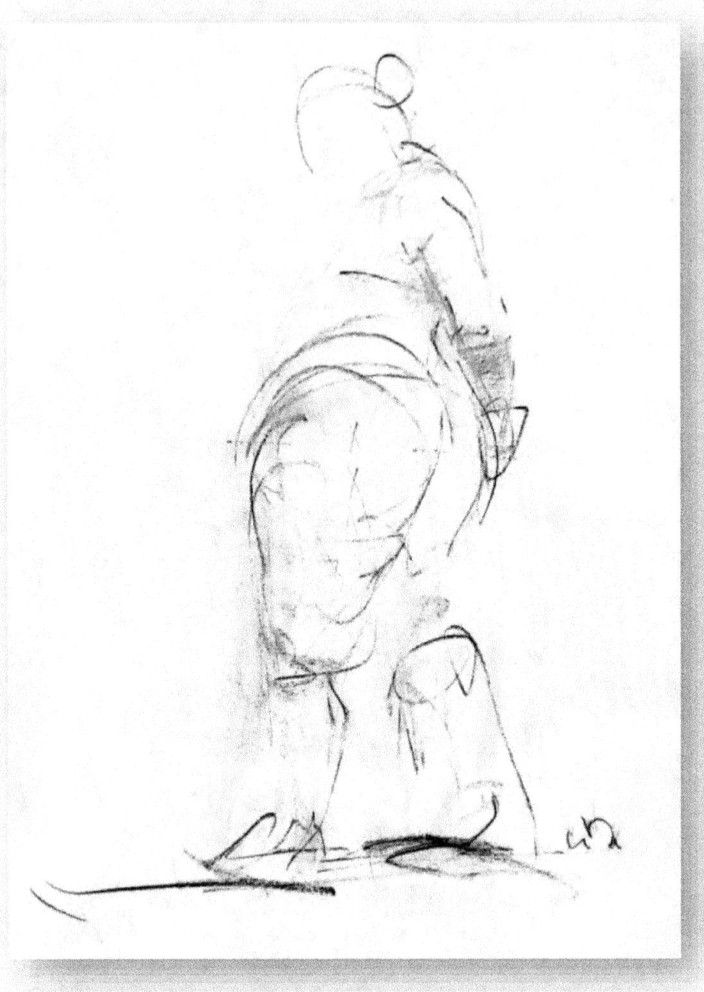

Figure 14 Leaning Female Figure

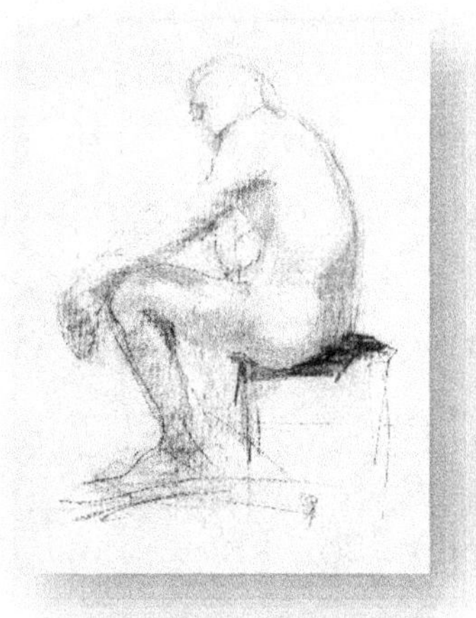

Chapter 12

Rhythm, Movement, Gesture

Flowing Figures in Motion

The masses of the body create its rhythm. The body's rhythm and structure interrelate. No surprise here. Rhythm refers to the energetic flow and the symmetry it creates.

The body's rhythm also depends on where the waist is. The waist is the smallest part of the torso. Anyone drawing the figure must know where the waist is. And that is true even for drawings that do not show the entire figure.

Keep your knowledge of the body and your imagination active, alive. See the entire body, its related masses, even when drawing a portrait, for example. The head relates to other masses, and those masses move certain ways to enable the head to appear a certain way.

The rhythms of the body's side view are important to know. When you know them, you know what to expect. That helps you see.

Outlines, light and shade, and colors, establish rhythm, all via balancing the body's masses through interaction of the inactive and the active sides that create a symmetrical flow throughout the pose.

The rhythm of the body always suggests movement. Movement relates to body mechanics. How the body moves, twists, bends, pulls and pushes furnishes the artist with endless studies. All movements in the body coordinate different body parts. Muscles integrate with one another; they actually shapeshift as they move. When muscles contract, they affect the underlying structure, the bones. Consider that everything is about to move. For example, as one arm moves, so does the corresponding shoulder blade.

What you are drawing is the body's harmonized action.

In general, movement is complex, making it even more important for artists to know human anatomy. Of course, such knowledge amplifies when comprehending details of muscle movement and so on. In this sense, drawing constitutes peeling an onion, though the analogy is not entirely correct because what renders human form starts with the skeletal arrangement you cannot see.

The muscles, tendons, and ligaments that move skeletal masses work in tandem with another opposing muscle. Refer to the section on Masses and Centers for a quick refresher. In all movements of the figure, there is a stronger, often more angular side and a complementary softer or passive side. The two work together, creating a subtle flow of form that is in a state of change and elusive. This creates harmony in movement.

To communicate the subtle flow of movement just described, the artist may render many study drawings. Sensitivity to the model, the body's form, and its expression may be the ultimate result of putting in this work and effort.

How to draw movement?

Capturing movement is an artistic challenge. It is difficult. Countless artists have spent years studying movement and how to draw it. Locomotion. The wonderful New York artist Isabel Bishop's *walking* drawings and paintings show the challenges and innovations involved.

Motion of any kind shifts the form(s) in front of you. When the model moves, you will see certain parts of the model, not others. Forms might overlap, to a small or large degree. The changing perspectives this movement produces—as you are more stationary at your easel or on a drawing bench— leads to foreshortening.

I addressed foreshortening and how to capture these forms in the previous chapter, and now are going beyond this with our intention to depict a form in motion.

Capturing movement starts with forms that turn, twist, and bend and create both rhythm and weight in the process. The forms' volume, helped by light and shade, give the illusion of movement in a drawing.

With any movement, the muscles connecting the body's masses contract, shorten, expand and bulge. This affects the forms you see; there will be parts that overlap or interlock. As this happens, the outline changes.

The major masses—head, chest and pelvis—themselves are immovable. Their symmetrical arrangement and balance produces no movement, while these masses show movement when they turn, twist, and bend backwards or forwards. When that happens, observe how the side opposing the twists, turns and bends lends the figure a subtle, gentle flow. The sides, far from being independent of one another, work together and effect harmonious integration of the entire body.

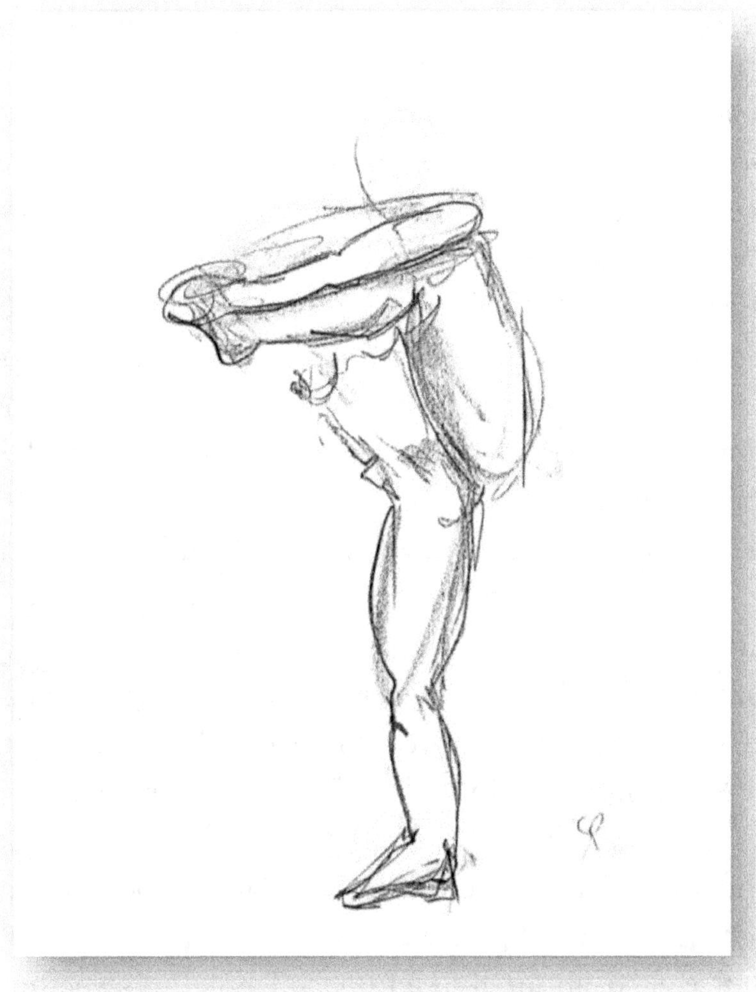

Figure 15 Quick Sketch of a Balanced Figure

The rhythm and the always implied movement in the figure now lead us to gesture. One way to understand gesture is as the natural result of rhythm and movement. Consider it as the attitudes and expressions that result from both.

Gestures, although always present in multiple ways, can be momentary, fleeting. Yet, the artistic capture of it is a wonderful asset in comprehending and sustaining it.

Drawing ability and gesture closely link. A successful drawing emerges through sustained gesture drawing. The first marks of any drawing are light and gestural. Sustained gesture drawing adds more gestural layers, and all these layers lend the work cohesiveness.

Remember to keep your drawing flexible until it makes sense. The best part of gesture is doing it again and again. Gestural drawing encompasses constantly passing from one end or part of the body to another. The entire figure is its focus because it is one energetic unit that moves. Don't hesitate when drawing the gesture. Doing so stifles your drawing. It will fall apart.

The Natural Way to Draw by Nicolaides guides students to extract the gesture.

Get excited about the action and put the structure right behind the action. How to do that?

Gesture is dynamic and represents movement in space. Gesture unifies a drawing. It is the essence of figure drawing. Without it, any drawing looks stiff and lifeless. When drawing the gesture of a pose, think of it as capturing the energy and flow of the pose. Do so in as few strokes or marks as possible. Details have no place here. They follow later.

As you start your drawing, draw a simple gestural mark or line that denotes the body's attitude. For example, if the model's body leans a certain way, capture that movement and attitude, then build on it with additional gestural marks and put in the body's structure. You must be able to feel the gesture in your own body. Yes, drawing is that visceral.

Always build your work sensitively, lightly versus with heavy, dark marks that are difficult to mold and correct. Perhaps consider this part a fun dance in which you engage with the model in front of you without ever touching the model. There is immense beauty in this process. And when you do so, you capture the pose on your paper and to show and express what YOU see.

This takes time, concentration, focus, and meticulous attention. This only happens when undistracted by chatter and by details that do not (yet) matter.

When referring to gesture, remember that gesture drawings are

- Quick
- Often poses no longer than two minutes.
- Fluid, flowing sketches.
- Lend themselves to drawing a live model.
- Sustained gestures are those that define all drawings, no matter how long.

I believe drawing changes the brain. Drawing also makes you attentive. It makes you pay attention to what you are looking at which is not easy.—Milton Glaser

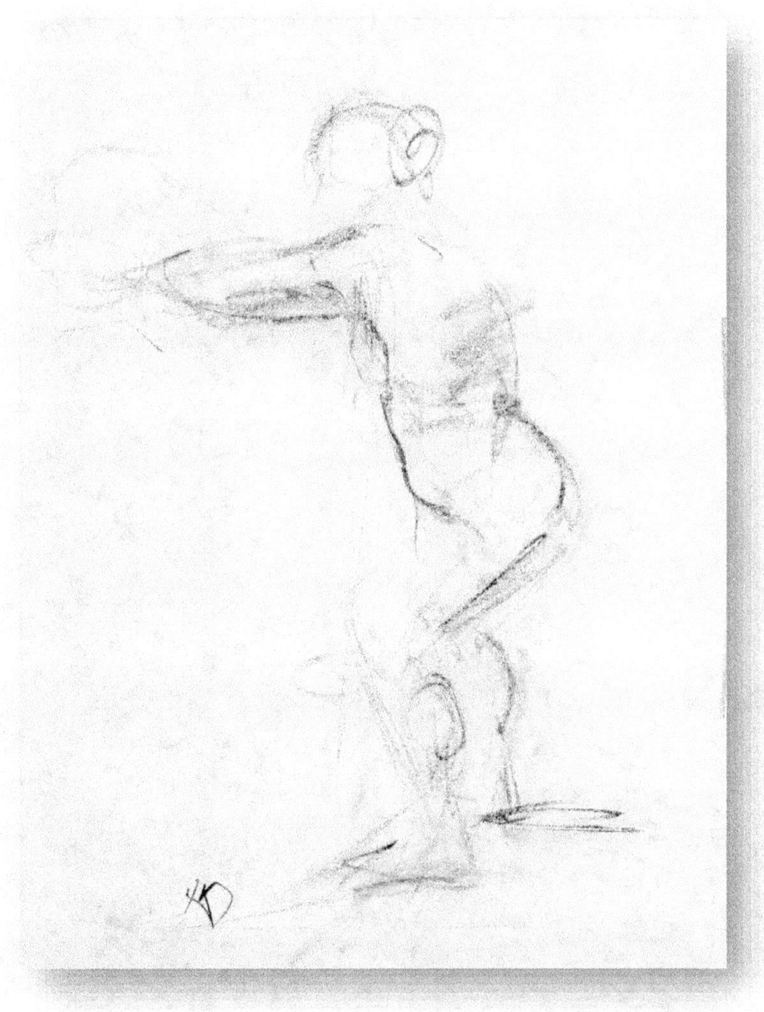

Figure 16 Quick Gestural Drawing

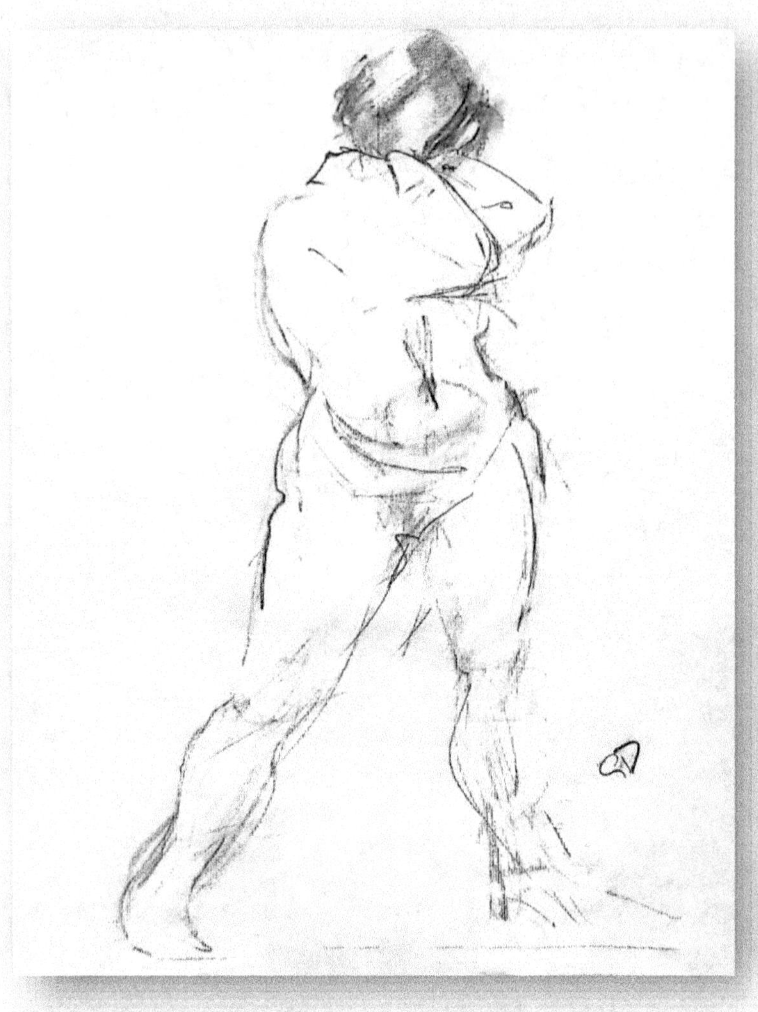

Figure 17 Gestural Drawing

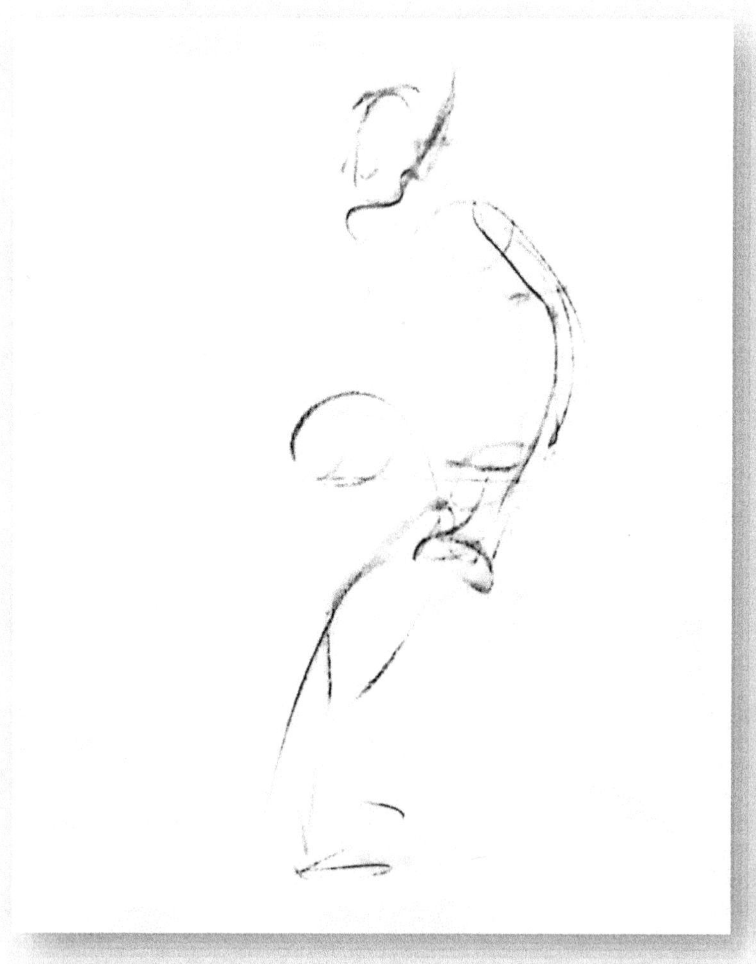

Figure 18 30-Second Gesture

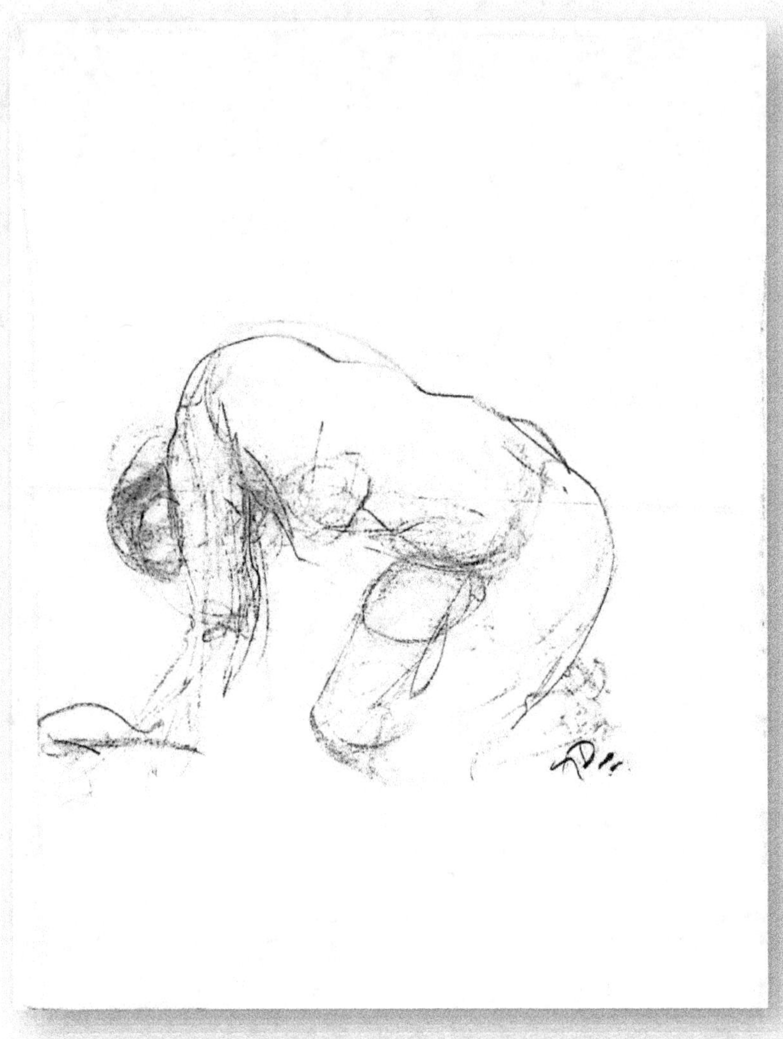

Figure 19 The Gesture of Movement

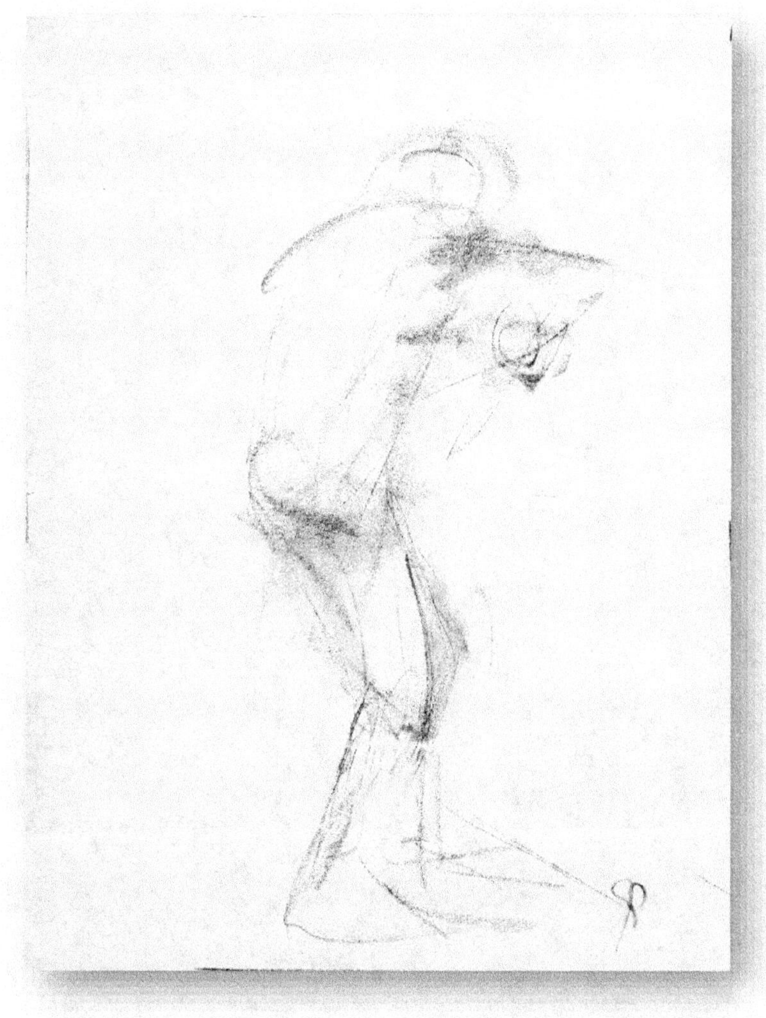

Figure 20 Gesture of a Standing Figure

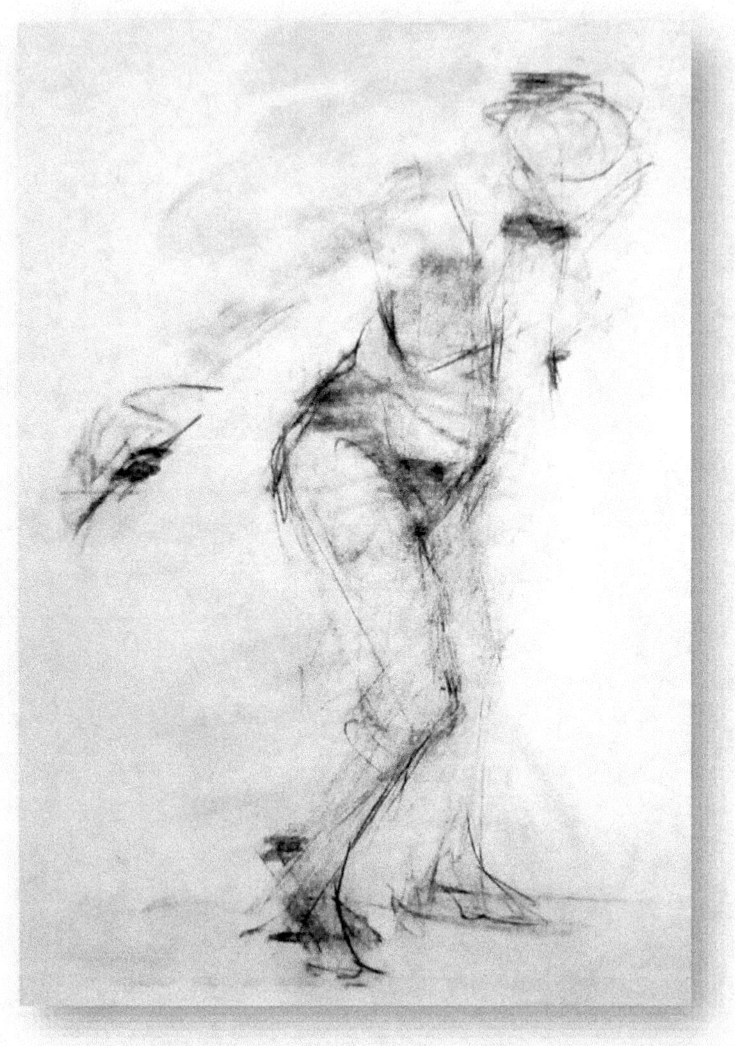

Figure 21 Gesture of a Movement

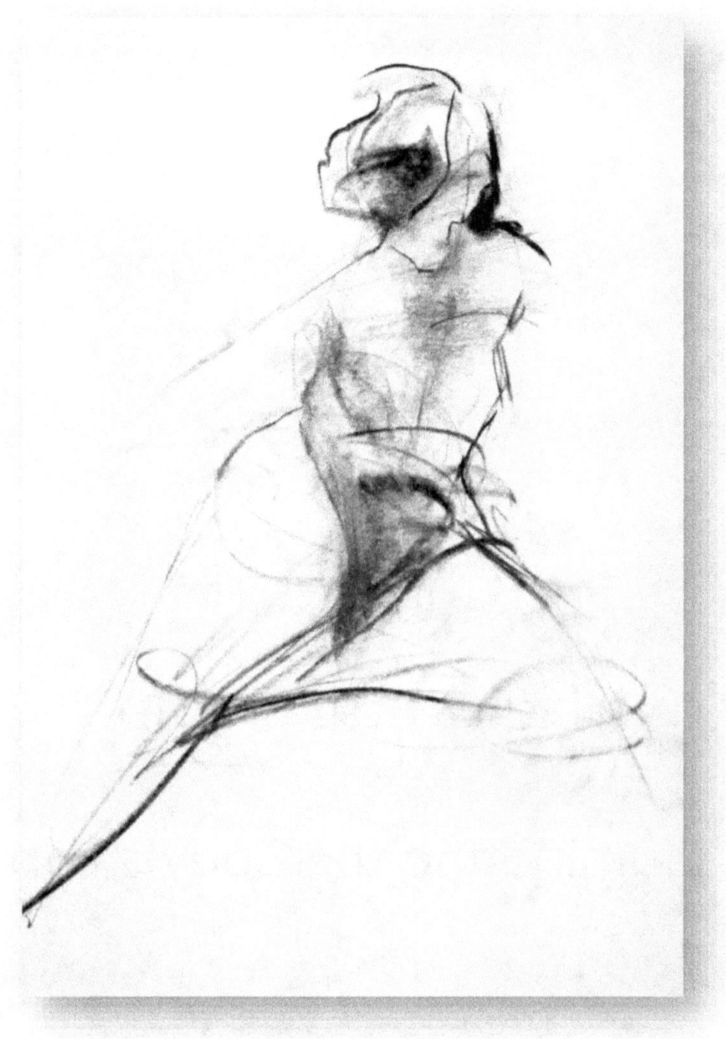

Figure 22 Implied Movement Gesture

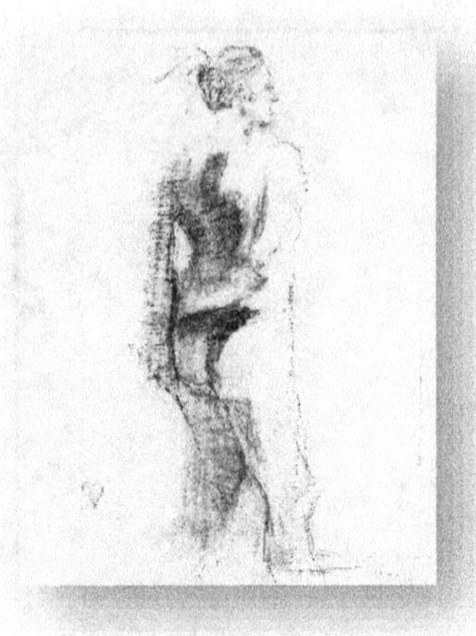

Chapter 13

Light and Shade

Illuminating the Body's Forms

Although light and shade in and of themselves do not make drawings, they are important in lending the drawing depth and solidity. When shading, you likely have a value scale. If not yet, now is the time to develop one. Value scales range from light to dark.

Values are relative because they depend on their surroundings. They illuminate the form and give it a sense of light. They model the form you see and also solidify the figure's appearance and its depth.

When first learning to draw, many artists engage in shading the figure evenly, also known as flat shading. It ignores the human form by making it a uniform, undifferentiated blob. In reality, the human figure is a complex collection of forms. Shade with that in mind.

In shading a drawing, make certain to shade so that there is a definite difference between tones. But use economy with tones and use only a few. Keep your shading simple and arrange them alternately.

As you apply shades to your drawing, eliminate areas of equal size or intensity immediately above another shaded area. The same applies to shaded areas that are side by side.

When light shines down on objects, cast shadows appear below them. They result from an object, including the figure, blocking light. One important thing to know about cast shadows is that they are darker than the shadows on the object itself.

Cast shadows have clearly defined edges closest to the form they abut and softer in areas of the cast shadow that are farther away from the object, in our case, the figure.

Depending on the light source or multiple light sources, how large they are, and on their set-up, cast shadows have differing qualities and appearances. All affect how and what you see of the model and the surrounding environment.

A picture must possess a real power to generate light, and … I've been conscious of expressing myself through light or rather in light.—Henri Matisse

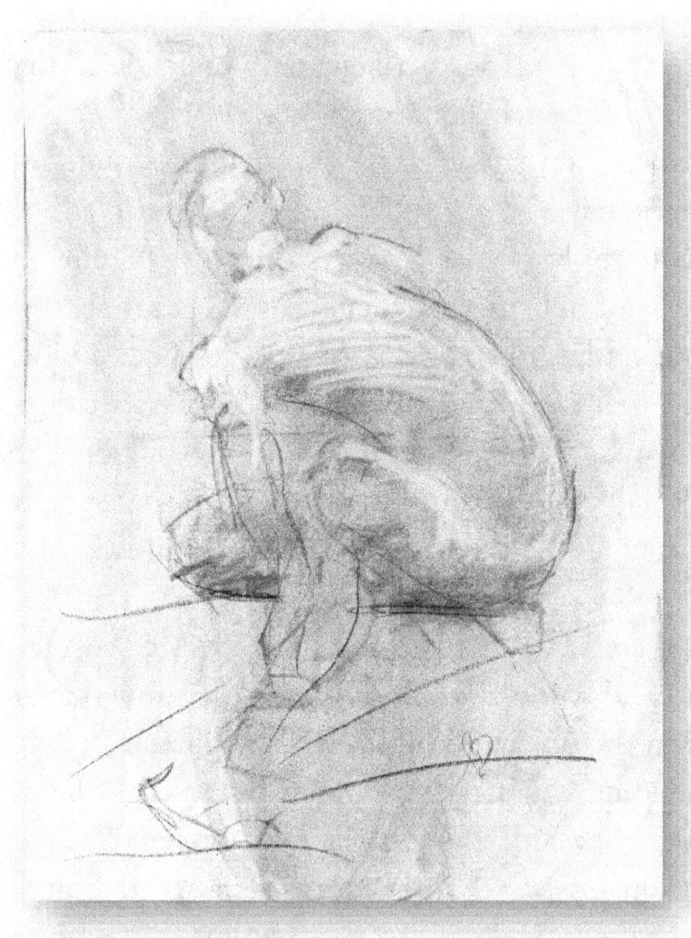

Figure 23 Capturing Light and Shade in a Quick Study

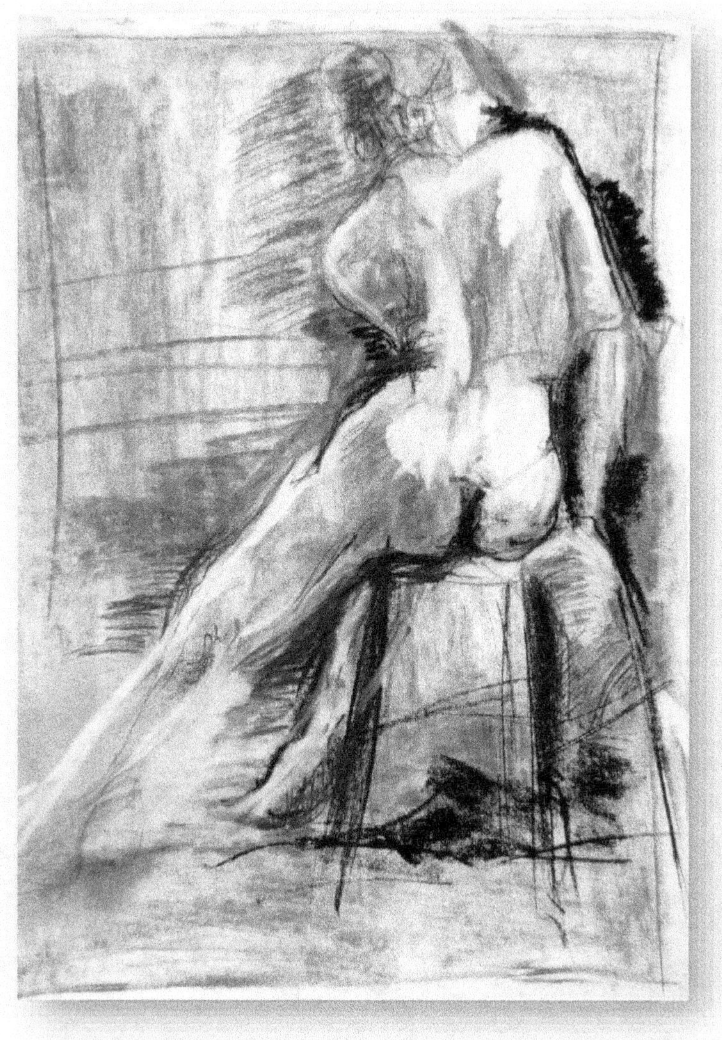

Figure 24 Using Various Techniques to Shade the Figure

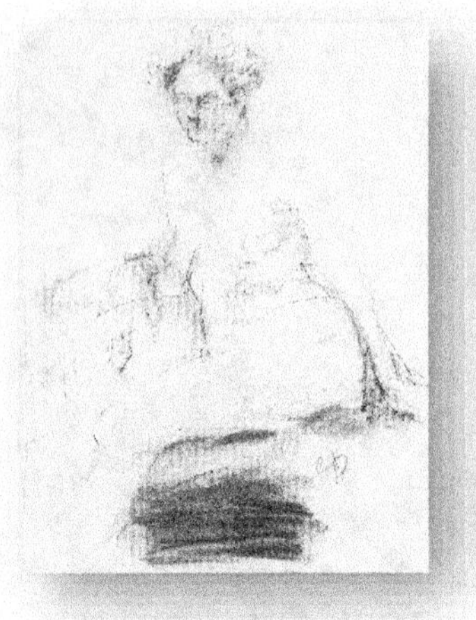

Chapter 14

Contour and Line

Outlining and Inner-Lining the Figure

Contour and lines are as important as the masses and centers discussed earlier. They help you see. They lend expression. No one line has the same expression as another.

The funny thing is that internal lines, those coming from the inside of the body, not those outlining it, in general, are much more interesting. They *feel* the subject. They draw tension and otherwise unseen connections. That means that there are contours inside the figure, not just on the edges of it.

However, contour drawing is useful in developing hand/eye coordination. That is especially true when your eye stays with the model while your drawing hand follows on paper what your eye sees. No peeking at the paper while contour drawing.

Contour drawing teaches the artist patience. It slows you down and allows imbibing the forms in front of you via all senses, not just the eyes. Draw what the person or thing in front of you is doing, rather than what it looks like. Even if your drawing looks nothing like the model, it is nothing to worry about.

It may help to know that a contour drawing comprises different planes, because the form constantly turns into space. That means that moving straight down in one form, maybe the torso, the leg, or the arm, is impossible.

Another valuable experience is that of contour drawing with your non-dominant hand. The results often astound because there is no internal expectation of something recognizable and finished. Plus, drawing with your non-dominant hand takes more time—and more attention.

I believe line, its variation and its beauty is a sculptural tool in an artist's arsenal. Lines communicate that a drawing is a sort of sculpture. Line determines form. As such, it clearly relates to contour drawing. However, the line is also different from contour drawing. Contours mostly serve to distinguish forms and the masses that belong to them, even though they may only be hinted at. Lines and their variations, on the other hand, often show more sensitive components and attitudes in a drawing.

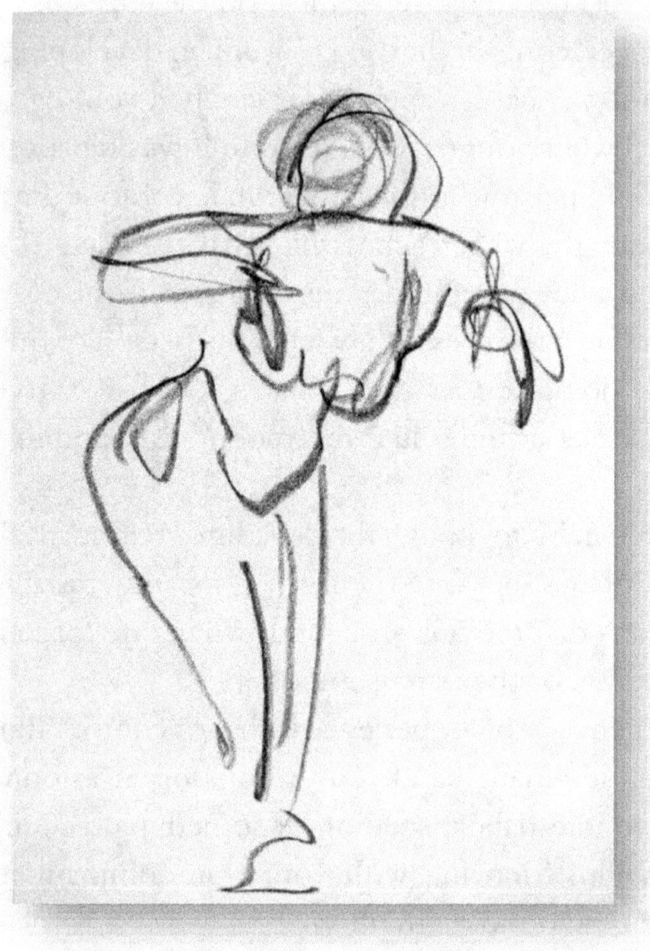

Figure 25 Contour Drawing

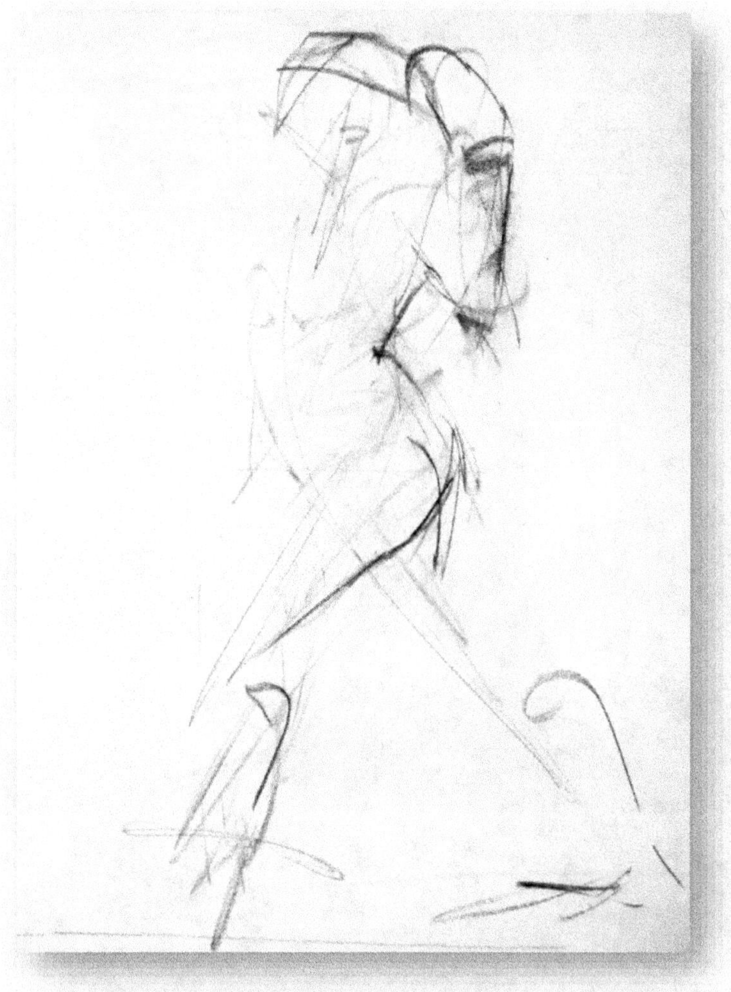

Figure 26 1-Minute Line Sketch

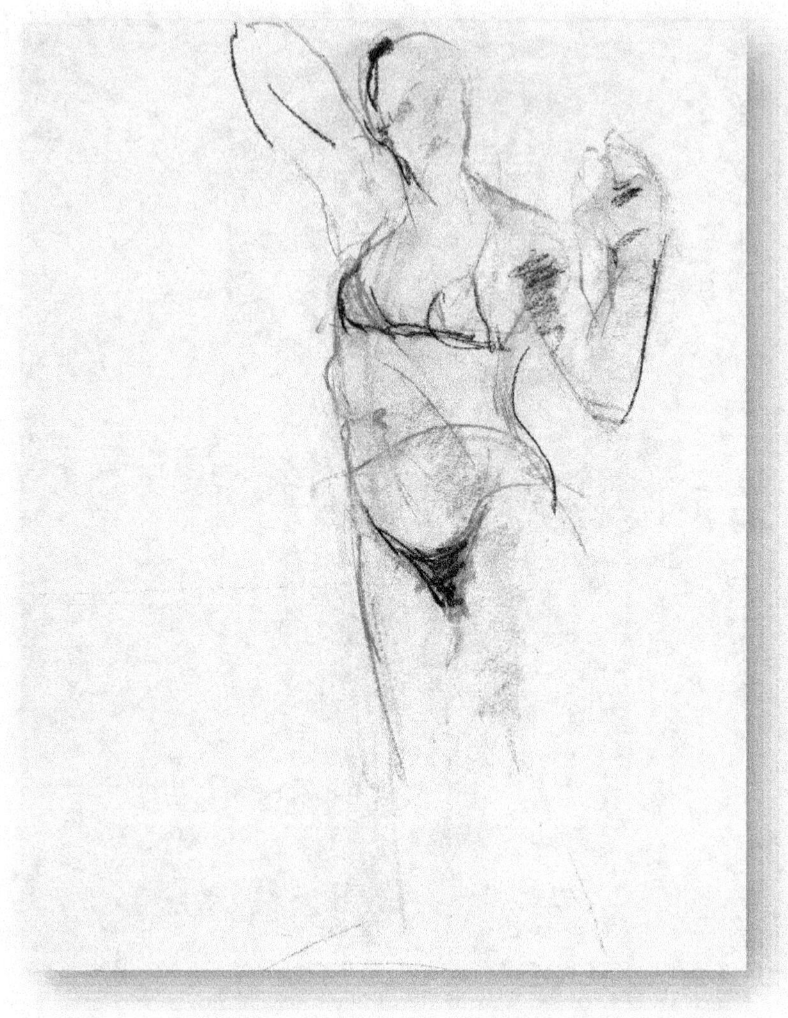

Figure 27 The Importance of Line

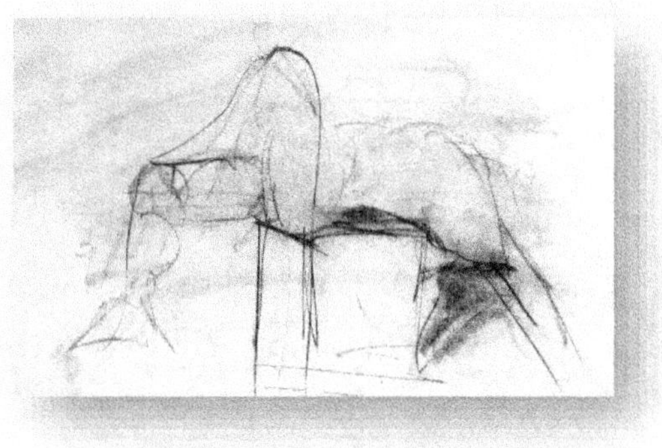

Chapter 15

Expression

Articulating and Imagining

Artistic expression refers to psychological, emotional, and spiritual components and messages in a work of art. Such expression can be socially significant, just as it can be offensive. It is a personal mark that stamps the artist's work.

While figure drawing records the model's pose, both the model and the artist, being human, have emotions, proclivities, and attitudes. These reflect in drawings and through artistic choices such as perspective, composition, material and color choices, abstraction choices, and more.

Consider artistic expression a language whose syntax may reveal the deeper levels of the psyche. This implies a symbiotic relationship between artist and model. This is as true for a onetime session as it is for long-standing work relationships between model and artist. In this context, the model in no uncertain terms may be an artist's muse.

While expression enlivens a drawing (or other media art works), it is a facet that comes into its own through the process of imbibing artistic fundamentals. These are the vocabulary which allows for artistic literacy. When established, such literacy sets you free to express and to do so deliberately and with integrity.

For example, the study of anatomy adds expressiveness to your drawings, in part because the underlying anatomy also imbues the drawing with dynamic elements. There is a constant interplay between structure, anatomy, design and expression in all great artworks. Nathan Goldstein was among the first to articulate this.

Further, drawing marks and line quality are expressive in their own right. And intentional distortion imbues expressive qualities, though this applies once you master the fundamentals.

All art forms, whether drawing, painting, writing, sculpting, dance, or any other form of creative expression possess transformative power. They meld intellect, intuition and feelings with technical know-how. They express your individuality and what you share with others at the same time.

Self-expression, communication through a medium like drawing, the ability to relate an inner world that may be multi-layered, discovery about who you are, and even releasing emotions, all belong to artistic expression.

Now, let's bring these very things into focus as they relate to figure drawing.

From doodles to stick figures to studies of say heads or hands to finished drawings of the figure, expression is a continuum. By that I mean, the more an artist learns and knows about the fundamentals you read about in this book or in any excellent book about figure drawing, the more your individual expression appears.

Also, know that drawings that convey expressive qualities often are recognizable through the ages. In them and through them, the viewer experiences emotions and the drawing's dynamic properties. I love drawing with charcoal and refer you to the wonderful charcoal drawings of Käthe Kollwitz (1867-1945) to experience the medium in the artist's compelling and beautiful way. Purely descriptive drawings, such as medical drawings, do not possess this quality.

All things mentioned in this section are so individual and demanding that no drawing exercise follows this section. Instead, go back to the other drawing exercises throughout the text and practice drawing. As you progress, periodically return to this section and re-read it. See whether it rings true as you press on in your drawing ability and in your ability to see.

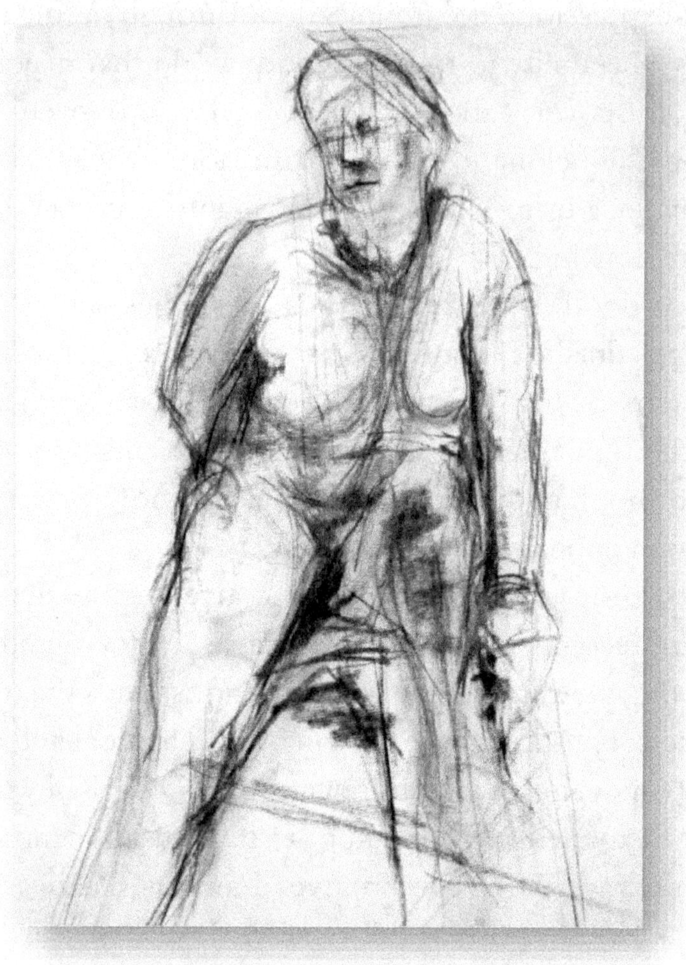

Figure 28 Seated Female

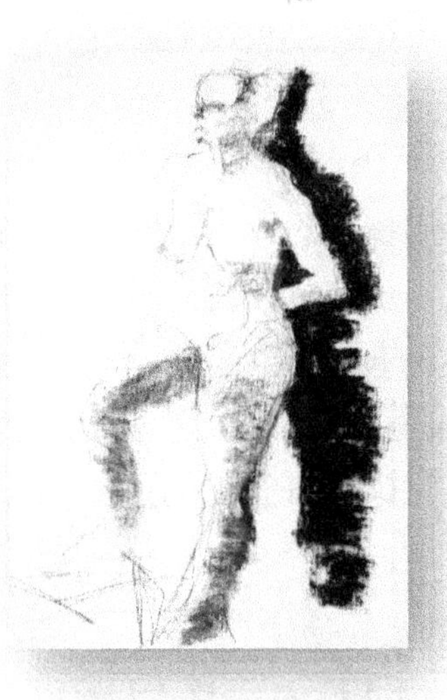

Chapter 16

Techniques

Boosting Your Drawing

Repertoire

Many drawing techniques can bring your art to life. I am listing many of them here, and suggest you take a basic drawing class either in person or online to learn more about them.

When working with any of these techniques, draw in a relaxed way, start lightly, vary the pressure on your pencil, and take your time. Experiment with varied strokes and with using the tip or the side of your pencil.

Okay, the techniques follow. Some of these have variations I omit here because the focus is on the essential ones.

- Cross hatching
  - Refers to parallel lines used for shading.
  - These lines may be tightly rendered or far apart.
  - This is a variation of hatching.
  - Either create light and shade and texture.

- Contour drawing
  - The outline of the drawing subject or object.
  - Once you draw the contour, you can add curved hatch lines.
  - The interior curved hatch lines follow the shape of your object.
  - The curved hatch lines are also known as coiling or circling.

- Blocking forms
  - Refers to drawing the forms of the masses first.
  - Correct proportions capture these forms.

- Blending
  o An important technique that softens your pencil strokes.
  o You can vary your pencil strokes and
  o You can vary your pencil strokes and make them side to side.
  o Use tissue paper, a Q-tip, a brush, or a paper stomp to blend lines. What you use depends on your drawing medium.
- Smudging
  o Great to use with softer media like charcoal.
  o Your fingers are the best smudging tools.
  o Smudging blends and softens.

- Stippling
  o Apply pencil dots in your drawing to render shade.
  o It is a different shading technique from others mentioned here.

- Rendering
  o Done with graphite pencil, you gently draw with your kneaded eraser to lift highlights off the page.

- Scribbling
  o Loose pencil marks on your paper.
  o Any direction you choose.

These are some basic drawing techniques. Naturally, you can combine them.

Using white chalk as highlights in a drawing might be a last resort for any artist, but the danger is that the drawing no longer reads. Its cogent, unified presentation easily can dissipate with the use of white highlights, or even entirely disappear.

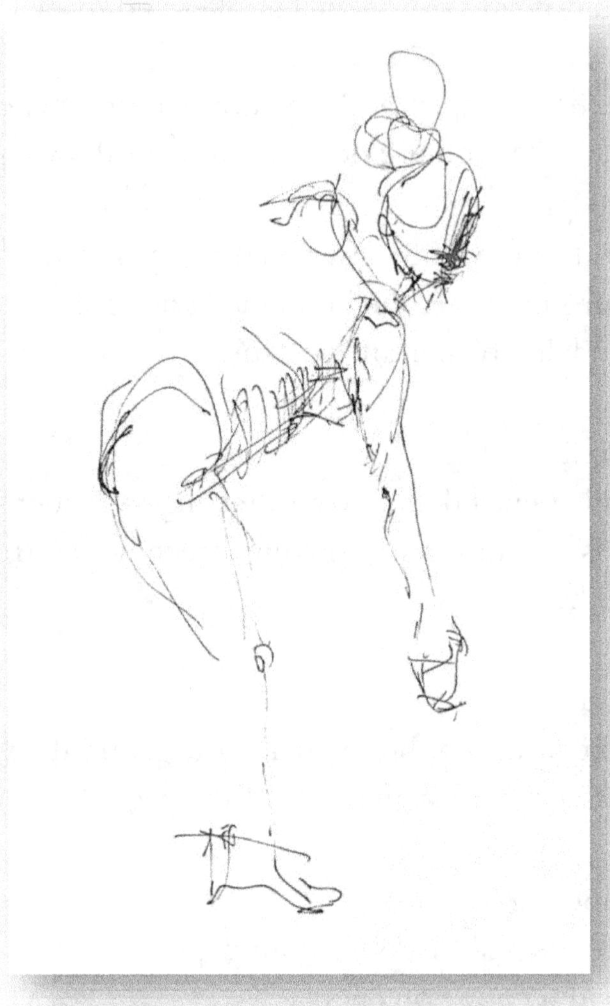

Figure 29 Inner and Outer Line Drawing

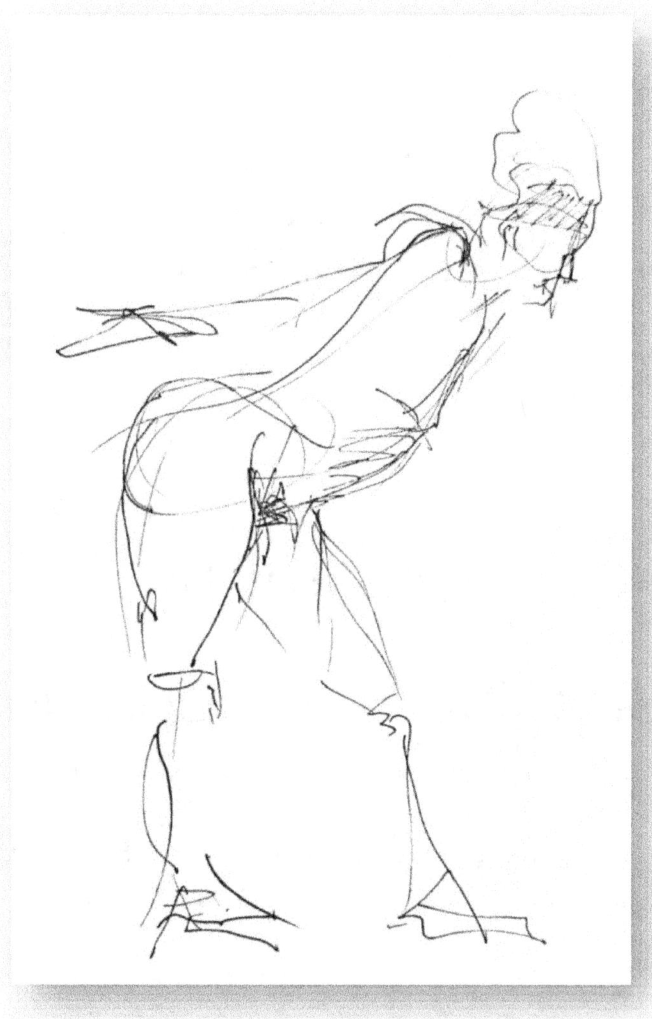

Figure 30 Line Drawing 2

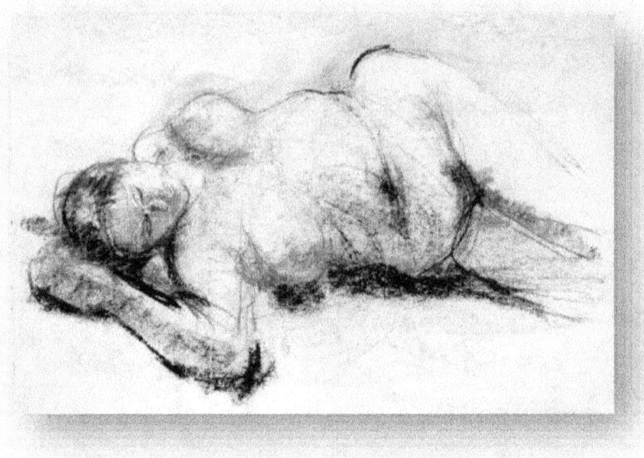

Chapter 17

Bringing It All Together

Drawing Grace and Beauty

All these factors must be present for a drawing to work, to communicate, to stand out, and to engage. Drawing the figure is a challenging task which requires preparation, willingness to learn and excel in the fundamentals, continuous practice, love of the craft, and immersion into the psychology of perception.

In figure drawing, the figure is a design, a machine, a flow, and an expression and revelation at the same time. How humans have done so for as long as we have existed is worthy of intense study. And that is because drawing the figure, alongside all art, is a record of innovation through the ages.

If this interests you, immerse yourself in the history of art to see this explanation corroborated.

You might notice that no mention of talent or drawing ability appears here.

That is because all humans are creatives, if they decide to develop in that direction. Talent is an overrated word, mostly connoting someone's innate gift. While prodigies exist, most of what others perceive as talent is, in fact, based on years of learning, absorbing, and practicing. In other words, on good old-fashioned hard work and never-ending application. If you commit to what's necessary to do this, your work will shine. That may be a tall aspiration, though for most eminent artists, this application and development has spanned decades.

But back to drawing the figure. A few tips follow:

- Begin with your composition in mind.
- Warm up and quiet your mind before you start.
- Slow down and feel out the pose in front of you.
- Abolish a piecemeal approach.
- Never begin a drawing with the details.
- Start and end with gesture.
- Keep your drawing flexible.
- Practice drawing geometrical shapes in perspective.

- Shade the forms.
- Practice foreshortened forms.
- Study anatomy and its application to art.
- Familiarize yourself with perspectives.
- Experiment with various materials and media.
- Learn all you can about the Masters.

As you progress on the drawing path, your passion, curiosity, and even wonder for drawing the figure will lead you forward. They are essential for any artist. Little happens without them.

Many eminent artists lived in difficult times with monumental challenges in their lives. Rembrandt van Rijn (1606-1669) is an example of this, but when you study his art his personal development, viewpoint, and passion are palpable and compelling. He was a master psychologist, this much his drawings and paintings reveal. That is as true for his work with models as it is for his many self-portraits. His life was filled with personal tragedy and adversity, the latter especially during his later years, yet his art saved him. What I mean by that is that his art was necessary for his soul to accept life and to flourish in spite of his circumstances.

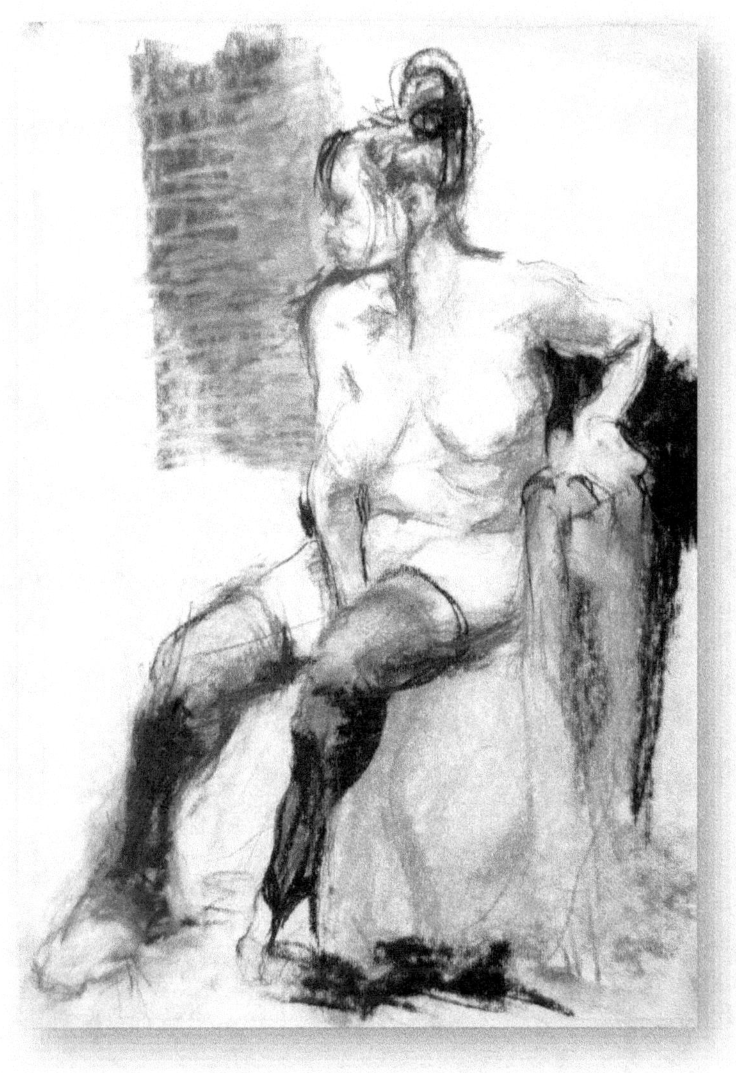

Figure 31 Finished Drawing

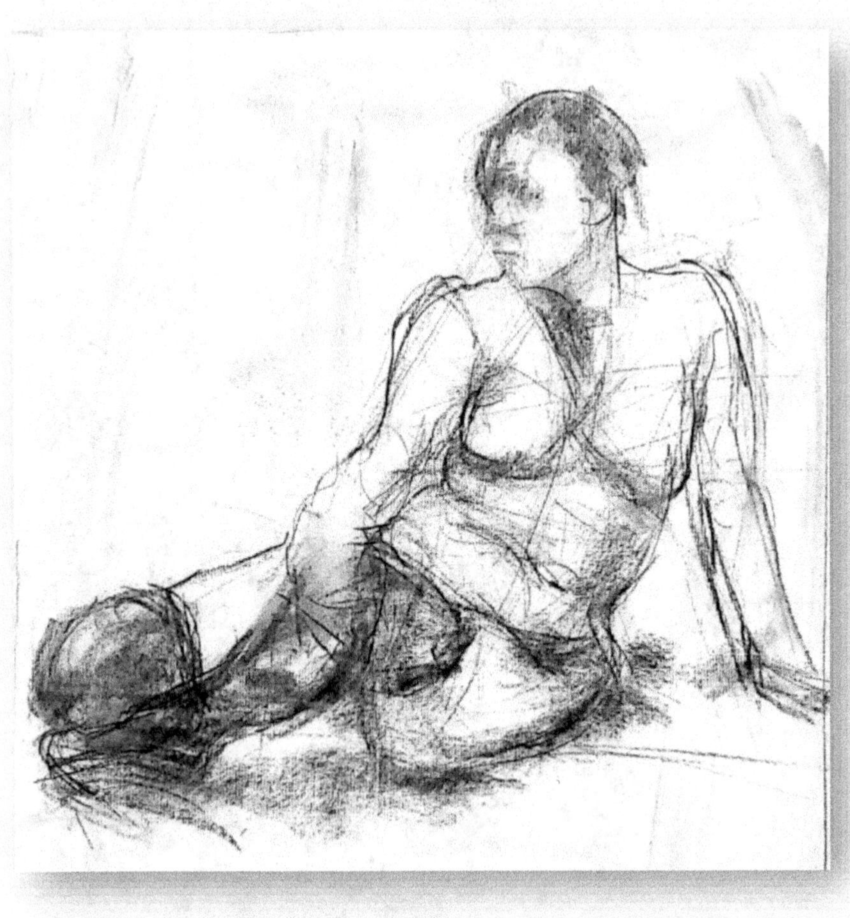

Figure 32 Seated Nude

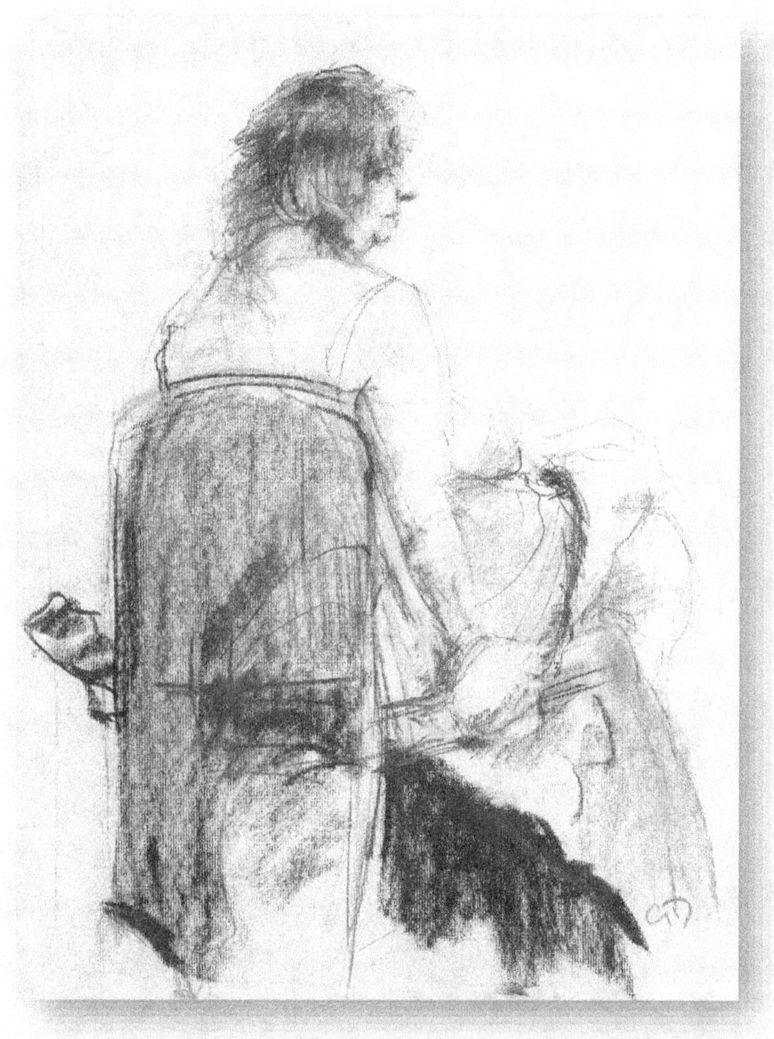

Figure 33 Seated Composition

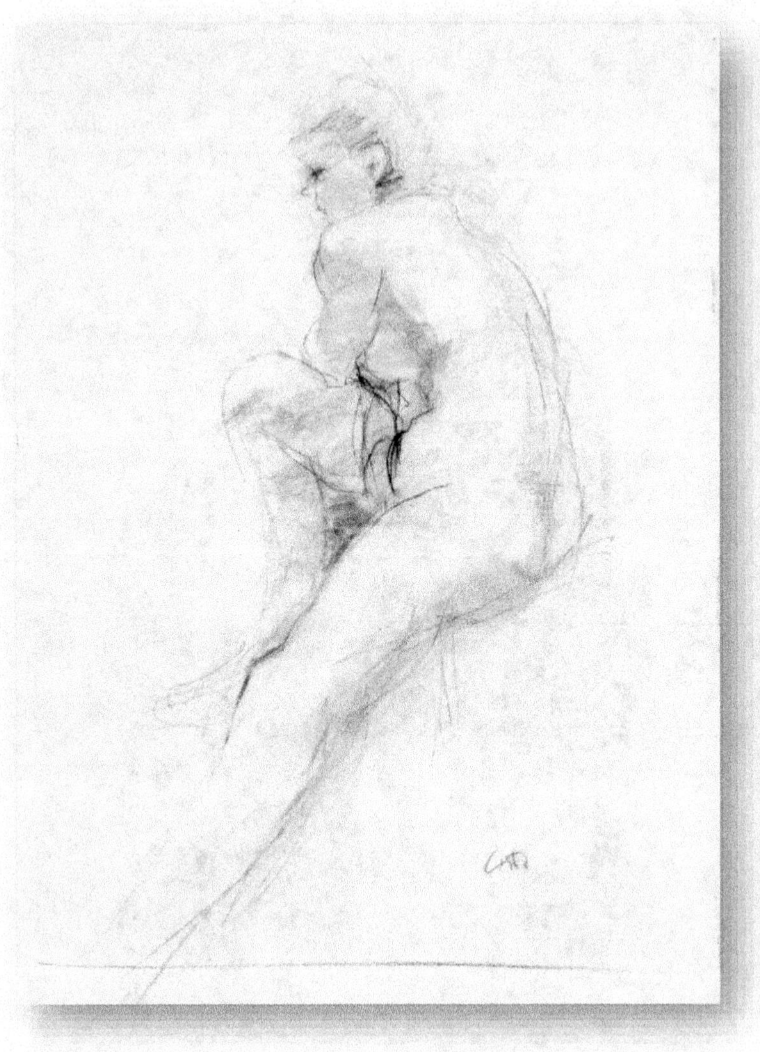

Figure 34 Seated Nude

The best figure drawings always reveal a congenial interaction among factors or structure, anatomy, design, and expression.–Nathan Goldstein

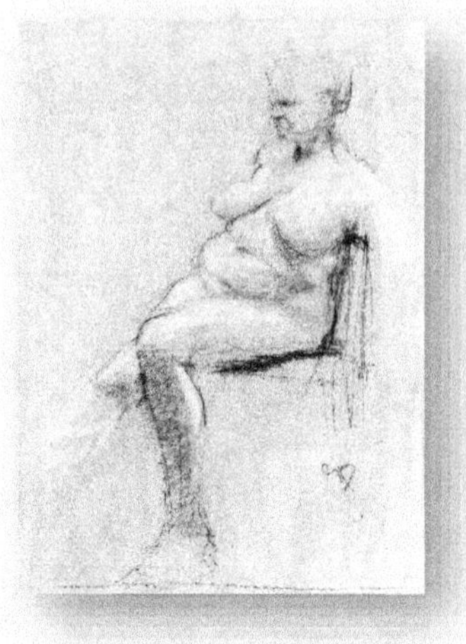

Chapter 18

Learning to Draw

Practice, Practice, Practice

Studying and drawing practice are the only paths available to anyone who wants to learn to draw. Commit to picking up a pencil, a pen, or other media of your choice, paper, and then put down the model's pose. Although I mentioned study, practice trumps all.

The book you hold in your hands or are reading in eBook format offers select exercises that follow most sections.

However, either take an art class facilitated by an excellent instructor, go online and find various exercises there, or consider the second volume of this title. That way, you have practice exercises to propel you forward on your drawing journey.

The ***Figure Drawing Workbook: Rhythm and Language of the Human Form*** provides you with a plethora of drawing exercises specific to the figure. The ***Workbook*** also delves into drawing media and how to set yourself up for success. Plus, its appendix provides you with additional resources. While the book you are reading now discusses some basics about media and set-up, the ***Workbook*** details them.

If you enjoy having all that information and the many drawing exercises in one place as an easy and accessible reference for you, the ***Workbook*** is of great help.

The exercises address many fundamentals you need to excel in to represent the human figure on a two-dimensional page, realistically, expressively, and imbued with your artistic vision. The exercises concern themselves with the many aspects discussed here.

Some are timed, others are not. Spend a minimum of three to five hours a week on developing your drawing skills, or more if you can. Reading books about drawing the human figure cannot and will not replace consistent and continual practice. The drawing exercises develop the perceptual, technical, and expressive skills and syntax that lend life, beauty, and communicative tenets to your drawings.

Another consideration to mention is this one: before drawing anything, walk around the model or object. See them from different angles and different vantage points, then find what interests you. See that in your mind's eye.

Then use your drawing arm and hand and start drawing the model in the air. You will have drawn the major centers and gestures before you ever commit them to paper. Doing so creates a memory of the pose in your body. Over time, your body memory will serve you well when drawing, though it is important to note that you must learn to trust it.

When overlaying your skeletal drawings with muscular layers, you model the human form. Next, observe how the skin envelops the skeleton, organs, and muscles. Consider the skin a sort of drapery.

The skin envelope effects surface forms and appearance. Fat deposits underneath the skin, which vary throughout the body, effect how these forms read. This means that artists must know and understand the structures beneath the surface. All surface forms offer clues about the structures and forms underneath them.

Visible torso forms often include the clavicles, the sternum, the rib cage, and the visible hollow at the pit of the throat.

When drawing the draped figure, the well-grounded artist communicates a deep grasp of the structure and anatomy of the human body.

In the words of Kimon Nicolaides,

There is only one right way to draw… It has nothing to do with aesthetics or conception. It has only to do with the act of correct observation, and by that I mean a physical contact with all sorts of objects through all the senses. If a student misses this step and does not practice it for at least five years, he has wasted most of his time and must necessarily go back and begin all over again.

This may sound harsh and imply less fun than what the terms art and artist generally conjure.

Spend three-hour blocks drawing. Turn off your phone and eradicate or minimize other distractions. The sooner you have a few thousand serious drawing hours under your belt, the better.

Making time to draw in such time blocks regularly is the only way in which to achieve mastery. Aim for mastery versus hobbyism, even if your art is a private pleasure.

In the process, banish perfectionist tendencies because they inhibit progress. As I mentioned elsewhere, welcome mistakes as stepping stones and valuable tools to learn. It is unrealistic to expect all your drawings to be masterpieces. All masterpieces arose from meticulous studies and preparatory sketches, most of which were less than masterful.

There is no failure. Only feedback.–Robert Allen

Enjoy the process of drawing and drop the expectations. If you continue your work and the various aspects important in drawing anything, you will improve.

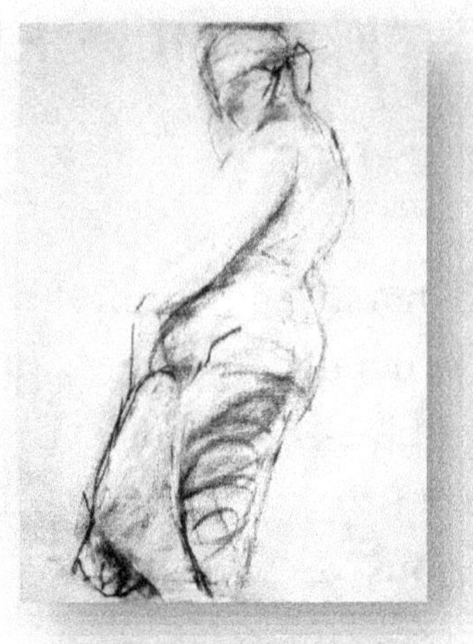

Chapter 19

Discipline and Focus

Supporting Your Creative Potential

You probably are wondering what discipline and focus have to do with figure drawing. Reframe any negative connotation you hold about them because without them no progress occurs. Discipline and focus enhance your artistic journey and make drawing a second nature activity. They elevate your art, and that is true for all levels of talent.

Discipline is the bridge between goals and accomplishment.—Jim Rohn

Discipline and focus go hand in hand. They provide the foundation you need to become a wonderful artist because they comprise applying yourself again and again to master the elements that feed into drawing. You read about them here, but only regular practice brings them into focus.

Regular practice, patience, and structured learning are all part of this. This sounds easy, but can be difficult if you have a day when you just don't feel like it. All of us have such days and those who do it anyway even when feeling this way, develop and engage discipline.

As a beginner, you are likely to practice basic shapes and forms. As an intermediate art student, you graduate to more complicated poses and lighting. As an advanced art student, you might push past styles and techniques you are accustomed to and attempt new, unfamiliar ones.

As you travel the artistic path, engaging in such discipline allows you to find your voice. Your art develops dynamically in this way. Those who view your work eventually glean your signature. They may appreciate it or not, but the journey is YOURS. Never underestimate the power of this.

Discipline allows you to develop focus, the ability to hone your observational skills. In drawing anything, including the figure, keen observation is paramount. It alerts you to subtle shifts in weight and balance, to capture the nuances of light and shadow on the human body, and to understand the relationship between different body parts.

This amazing ability lends your drawing a nuanced life because you see the details that infuse your drawing with energy and your authentic voice. At the beginning of this book, I mentioned that drawing the figure is a meditation and somatic wisdom. You may believe you are only drawing the model until you realize that any drawing speaks just as loudly about yourself.

Start getting into the drawing groove by:

1. Establishing a regular drawing schedule
2. Minimizing distractions, or even better, eliminate them.
3. Creating a quiet zone.
4. Warming up your body by stretching a little.
5. Take a few deep breaths.
6. Practicing mindfulness.
7. Tuning out your worries and focus on the model.
8. Beginning with short poses to capture underlying gesture.
    a. That means no details (yet)!
9. Drawing from memory. Often.
10. Joining a figure drawing class.
11. Finding a great instructor.
12. Being receptive to feedback.

Only continual, regular practice sharpens visual understanding, reinforces visual vocabulary, and fosters accuracy. Practice also allows you to improve your speed when drawing. Another invaluable asset in learning to draw with skill and panache is patience.

Patience and practice are integral to the ability to capture mood, the rhythm and language of the human form, and to send visual messages.

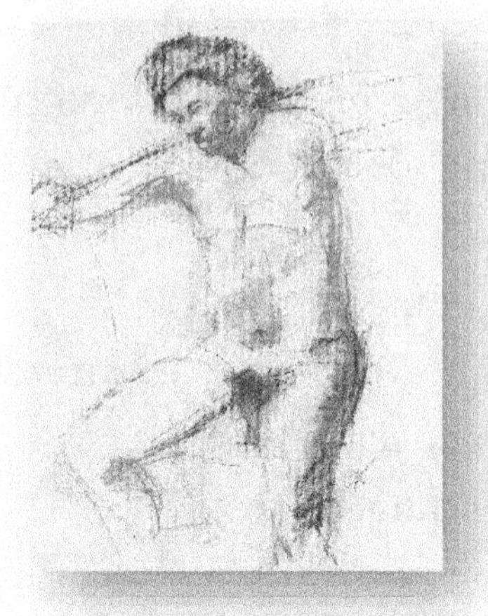

Chapter 20

When Is a Drawing Finished?

Elevating Your Art

The journey from sketch to finished drawing is interesting and subjective, yet there are telltale signs for finished drawings. They may include refined details, a composition that works, final touches, such as shaded areas.

Finishing a drawing can be a rewarding process!

Here are some steps to help you complete your artwork effectively:

- Step Back and Assess: Take a moment to look at your drawing from a distance. This will help you see any areas that need more detail or adjustment.

- Refine Details: Go over the areas that need more definition. Add textures, highlights, and shadows to enhance depth and realism.

- Clean Up Lines: Erase any unnecessary guidelines or smudges. You can also darken or refine the lines that are essential to the drawing.

- Color and Shading: If your drawing includes color, add it carefully. Use layers of color for depth and consider the light source to create realistic shading.

- Final Touches: Add any last details that can enhance the overall look. This could include small highlights, patterns, or additional elements to balance the composition.

- Sign Your Work: Don't forget to sign your drawing! I also date my drawings.

- Consider Presentation: Think about how you want to present your drawing. You might frame it, scan it for digital use, or display it in another way.

- Take a Break: After you finish, step away for a while. Coming back later can give you a fresh perspective on your work.

- Turn your drawing upside down and look at it from this new perspective. Doing this can help you make a better decision about whether your drawing is complete.

- Get constructive feedback from your instructor, if you have one. You may, of course, ask others for their feedback as well. Just know that their feedback may be off the mark, unless they understand what goes into an artwork. And never take feedback personally.

The danger of overdoing corrections is immense, and these can ruin your drawing. Knowing or rather sensing, when your drawing is complete can be a daunting task. It is a personal choice.

You decide when the drawing is complete, but your decision about that must come from your knowledge of all important elements that flow into a drawing. Yep, the fundamentals.

In Robert Henri's *The Art Spirit*, he states to stop drawing when you are done with a drawing. That sounds easy enough, yet it is a personal internal signal, one that only practice and experience bring.

Of course, even finished drawings have imperfections. You must be okay with that because perfectionism may well lead you to overwork the piece. I have suffered from this affliction myself and ruined artworks that way. Then beyond resurrection and relegated to the artwork graveyard, the only viable lesson from this is being more accepting of some imperfections to keep the work vibrant and alive.

Err on the side of stopping before you make corrections that lead to overwork. That's often just a little before you would naturally stop. It is a powerful decision point. It might help you know that how long you draw has almost no relationship whether a drawing is done.

Some fellow artists I know are afraid of mistakes and failing. No one wants to make mistakes or to fail, of course, but in their cases, some decide never to finish a drawing. That approach only leads to many unfinished drawings, and it hampers necessary learning. It also thwarts an artist's self-confidence.

Whether you succeed or not is irrelevant, there is no such thing. Making your unknown known is the important thing.—Georgia O'Keeffe

---

Let's return to the topic of deciding when a drawing is finished. For figure drawing, accurate proportions are one consideration that determines whether your drawing is complete.

Ask yourself the following questions to figure out whether your drawing is finished:

- Have you used the medium to its fullest?
- Is the composition balanced?
- Is it harmonious?
- Do you have a clear focal point?
- Is the drawing stylistically complete?
- Does it convey a visual message that is discernible?

- In case you use color, does it contribute to the drawing's mood?
- Does the color scheme work?
- Does the work carry visual weight?
- Is the value range complete?
- Does the drawing display a full range of values?

All aspects congeal in a complete drawing, although every artist deliberately, often intuitively chooses emphases. That means an artist may use only lines, for example, and forego values. However, all other elements in the drawing still must work well together.

As with all subjects and interests, the time and attention drawing demands mean mistakes are inevitable. Mistakes serve as long as you learn from them. Keep on going and regularly review your work to see what is amiss. Then correct them to the best of your ability.

Some mistakes are habits that only show up over time. For example, drawing details before the structural aspects of the drawing are complete. Watch out for those.

Make as many mistakes as necessary to improve your drawing ability and your work. The sooner they happen, the better. I have made thousands of them and so have the masters. Mistakes are hardly a reason to give up; instead, they are reasons to buckle down to address and correct them.

You will create hundreds, no, thousands of drawings. I hope that excites and inspires you as much as it does me.

Initially, your ratio may be one good drawing to a hundred. As you continue, this ratio is likely to change. All good and great work stems from practice. The effort is ongoing. It may and usually does take many years to develop excellent practice. There are no shortcuts. Any artist must put in the work!

Keeping your drawing flexible is invaluable in this regard. Always start with a light touch. You may wipe down the drawing and start over on that same drawing page. To do so means that some of the old marks are still on the paper, however faint they may be. They help create an organic architecture for the drawing and often even lend the drawing depth.

One stroke, mark, and line can make the difference in finishing a drawing. But which one is it going to be? Practice economy and study your drawing over several days without touching it.

A beautiful mark is an expressive mark, a mark executed with sensitivity. Such sensitivity arises from all the aspects you are reading about here, including artistic vision. All marks you make contain your style.

I wanna see what you got…the complete expression of you in the moment. No restrictions…how you feel.—Savion Glover

---

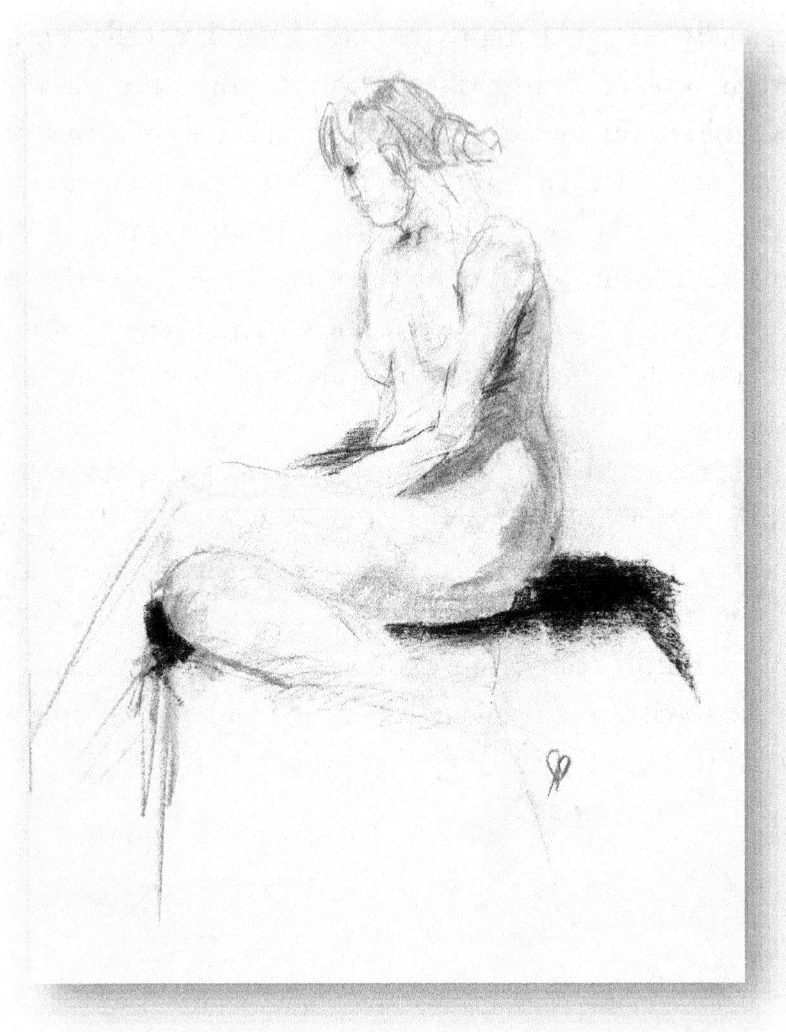

Figure 35 Finished Piece Charcoal and Chalk

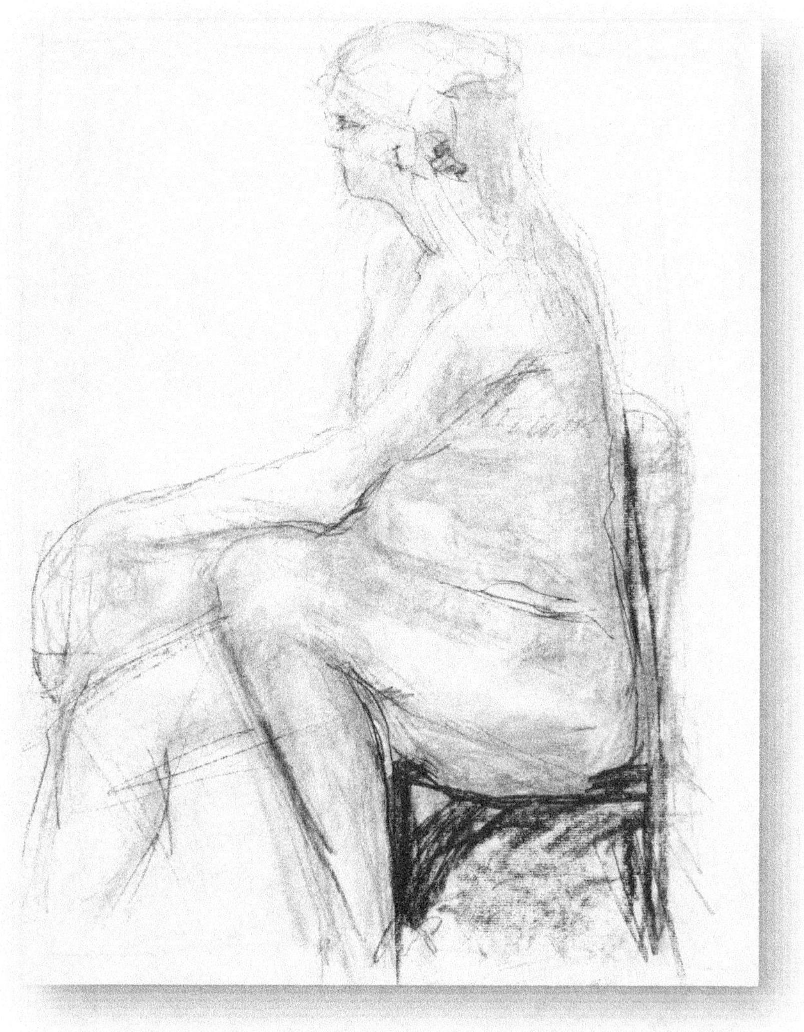

Figure 36 Finished Drawing

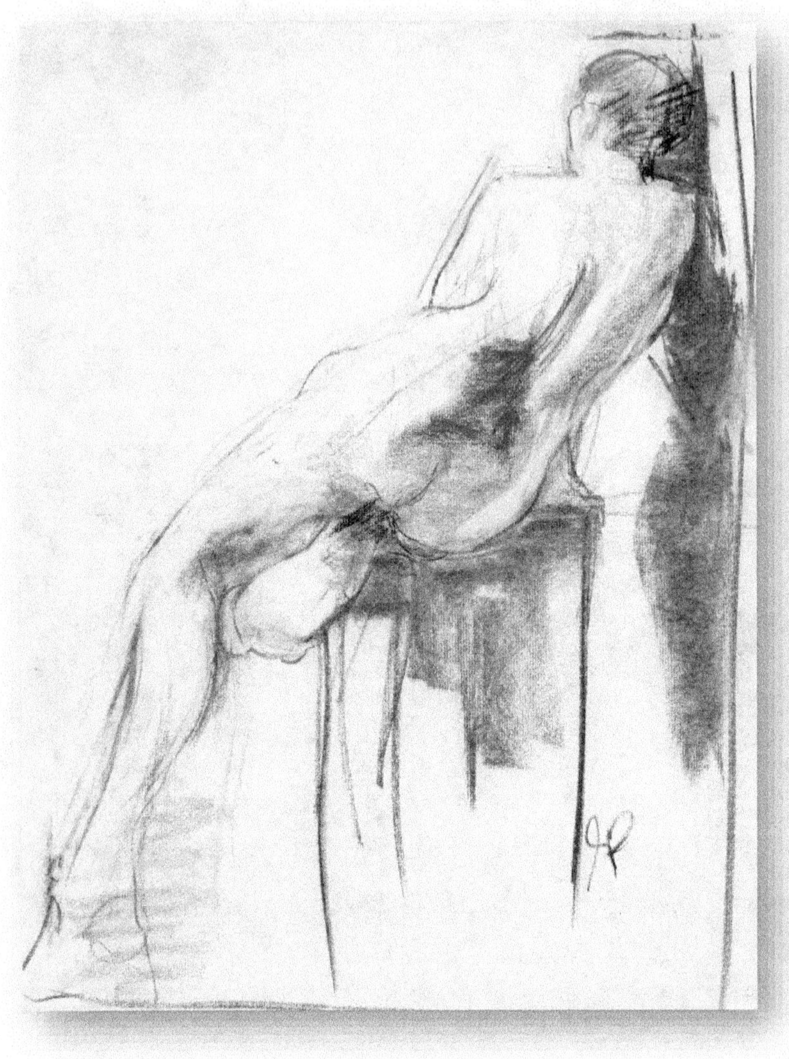

Figure 37 Finished Piece

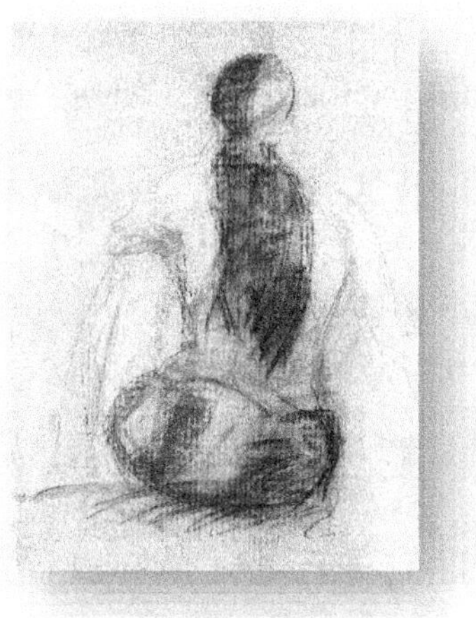

Chapter 21

Away from Drawing

Never a Dull Moment

As you can see, drawing comes to you through life or, more accurately, through keen observation. The mundane becomes extraordinary in that process. In that sense, drawing is a spiritual process. However, that is only true when observation and vision align and when you develop the many technical facets discussed here.

Invention has no place in this until the artist masters all these facets, one by one.

You are becoming a keen observer of objects and people around you, right?

As you do so, you may not always be able to draw what you see immediately. Or maybe you forgot your drawing journal, pencils, and pens. Take in what you see with great attention. Then attempt a memory drawing of what you are seeing now later.

Even when in class, with the model posing, you can employ drawing from memory. But with the model in front of you, just sit or stand without drawing and observe the model and the pose. After the pose is complete or even when no longer in the model's presence, draw it from memory.

This may be quite difficult at first. Maybe your mind just goes blank. If you trust yourself and stay clear of your analytical mind trying to direct you, you are apt to tap into your subconscious mind and produce a drawing. The drawing might look different than you thought it would or should, so engage a no-judgement attitude. Keep going and practice memory drawing regularly to test your powers of observation. As time passes, you might be surprised at how informative and fun memory drawing is.

When drawing from memory, it is great to keep those drawings "short," meaning to spend only a little time on them. When the model moves from pose to pose during 20-second, 30-second, or 1-minute poses, observe drawing nothing, then after several such poses go to your paper and draw as many of the poses you just observed as possible.

Study the masters. Leonardo DaVinci, Rembrandt, Picasso, Michelangelo, Daumier, Degas, Ingres, Mary Cassatt, Georgia O'Keeffe, Isabel Bishop, and so many others. When you study the masters, you enter their world and immerse yourself in all facets of art.

You will learn about perspective, drawing conventions of the times they lived in or are living in, composition, capturing movement, materials and color, and any master's particular interests and drawing idiom.

This means doors open for you and your work. As you contemplate the art of those before you or your contemporaries, tap into their knowledge. Perhaps imagine a conversation with them, based on the art and artists you study, or when you are studying one of their artworks by drawing it yourself. What fun is that?

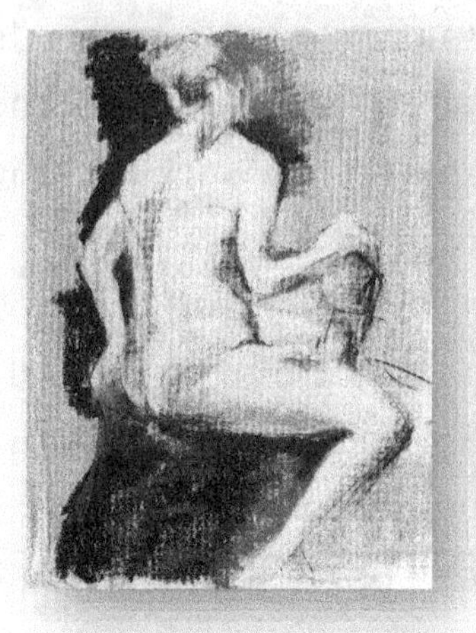

Chapter 22

Go to a museum

Perfecting Your Artistic Skills

Museums are treasure troves. They offer windows into art of all times. Exhibits usually are curated, which means the accompanying text to an artwork on display offers insights. These include insights into the artists, their process, their proclivities, their interests, their lives, their media, their times, and even their audience or the audience for which they drew or are drawing.

When contemplating an original artwork right before you, note the difference between them and artwork reproductions, such as in books, or on postcards and posters. The emotions or intellectual responses the original elicits in you are also instructive. How an artwork conveys its visual message may inspire new ideas and drawing approaches in your work.

Museums are wonderful places to sketch and draw as well. They often have benches or seats that allow you to spend considerable drawing time, though standing and drawing also work. Know that few museums allow easels in their galleries. Some museums have stools available for anyone wishing to draw in their galleries. Ask whether the museum you visit offers this.

One important thing to keep in mind is that museums are guardians of the artworks they house. Their staff watches over the galleries to protect them from any vandalism. For this reason, it is safest for you to bring your sketchbook, pencils, and colored pencils. Charcoal and pastel are too dusty, and galleries do not allow paints.

Once at the museum, find a piece that speaks to you, take out your drawing journal, and draw it. You might make notes about the work as well. You could also alter your approach and select an artwork you think you dislike.

Copying this piece might give you additional valuable insights. I have often found that there was more to appreciate about the piece than I believed to be there before drawing a copy of such a work.

*Those who do not want to imitate anything,
produce nothing.—Salvador Dali*

In addition, museums are full of people and as they move about to view an exhibit, you can easily draw quick sketches of them.

Drawing in museums expands your appreciation of other artists and of the artwork on display. Besides, when copying a drawing or painting into your sketchbook, you create internal visual memories. In effect, you expand your visual vocabulary so that you can call upon it later.

Art instructors and even museum event staff often offer sessions or classes in museum drawing. Find out which museums in your vicinity have such classes and which art instructors offer them.

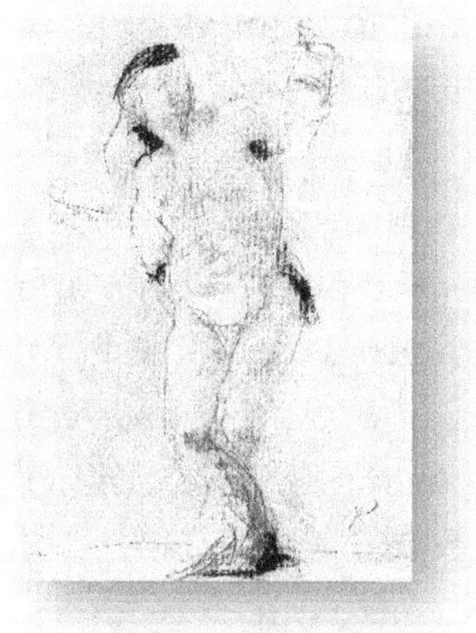

Chapter 23

Other places

Keeping On

Wherever you go, observe. Things of interest will appear. If you love a certain sport, dance, or music, attend a game, the ballet, the symphony, or an outdoor concert. These events are wonderful opportunities for you to observe and draw.

I often attend musical and dance events. Many of my studies, sketches, and drawings come from such events. For example, I used to go to the ballet with my sketchbook in hand and loved it. What I observed taught me so very much about gesture and movement.

You could go to the park or even a family event and draw. Where and what you draw is almost limitless.

While no official model poses for you unless your art class or you hire one, your models are ordinary people going about their routine activities. Of course, everyday people wear clothes, and that means your drawings show them. They also show the other layers beneath those clothes.

In this way, drawing people on the street, in a café, in a shop, in the park, or in many other venues supports your study of the fundamentals: anatomy, movement, light and shade, proportions, etcetera. Fabric and clothes covering the body must adhere to what's underneath them. Whole lectures and classes address drawing drapery. Find one, if available where you live.

You might also enroll in an anatomy course and read all art anatomy texts available. Artistic anatomy studies differ from anatomy studies for medical purposes. They concern themselves with understanding how underlying structural elements, such as the bones, muscles, tendons, and ligaments, affect surface forms and their appearance.

Another worthy study regards art materials, their characteristics, their effects, how to use them to the best advantage, techniques in applying them, and how they contribute to artistic expression. The section titled Settings and

Materials briefly considers them. Many good books about art media are on the market.

The accompanying **Workbook** to this book addresses art materials and figure drawing setting components and expanded figure drawing exercises.

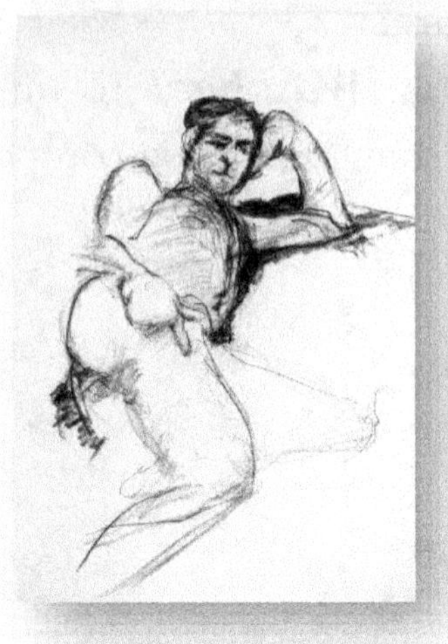

Chapter 24

Parting Words

Drawing fundamentals propel your artistic journey and expression. If you read this book in its entirety, your passion for figure drawing is clear. Figure drawing is a spiritual endeavor based on the study of life. This sustains artists as they excel in the technical aspects of drawing the figure. Artistic vision and technical know-how and panache form the tenets of expression. Both are necessary. They are interdependent.

Drawing is perhaps the most personal branch of the visual arts. It is a way to express the artist's response to life, its difficulties and pleasures, its mysteries, and its beauty.

Drawings are the artist's immediate, unvarnished responses to life and the world. They are a way to assess, comprehend, and depict our shared humanity, and they also attest to and reveal the forces outside ourselves and their influence on us. They often are intense for that reason. I consider them contemplations.

When learning to draw, know there always is more than what is apparent to the eye. Drawing, then, is a sensing of what is there, developed and built upon through the many aspects discussed in this book. It is the development of inner vision.

Put a different way, drawings are artistic expressions that originate with the layers of imagination and vision of the artist. I consider them somatic wisdom.Drawing can be cathartic.

Find out for yourself by putting some or all you have read here into practice and have fun!

An artist is not paid for his labor but for his vision.—James McNeill Whistler

---

If you found value in these pages and enjoyed them, please leave a review wherever you purchased the book. Perhaps also ask your local library to add this title to its shelves. Thank you!

You may also contact me at info@figuredrawing.life.

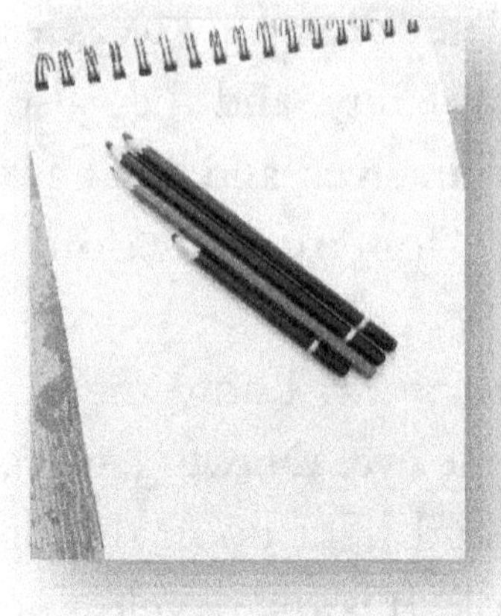

Chapter 25

Exercises

The drawing exercises that follow will get you going in your pursuit of learning and understanding figure drawing fundamentals.

No substitute exists for regular focused practice.

The *Figure Drawing Workbook*, the accompanying volume to this book, contains more drawing exercises for you.

1. Get a model of the human skeleton and draw it. Or draw the life size skeleton that often collects dust in most drawing classes.

Small skeleton models are available in art supply stores or online.

2. Draw the anatomy of different parts of the body: hands, feet, heads, the rib cage, and the many other bones and muscles comprising the human body.

3. Abstract the various forms and shapes of the body and the pose by drawing their corresponding geometrical shapes.

Remember that the body comprises many layers and that ALL of them interact with one another.

4. As you observe the model and the pose, draw abstract geometrical forms for the masses and limbs of the body. Account for masses and limbs you may not be able to see due to the pose. Doing so balances the figure and the composition. Find out how the forms relate to one another.

5. Draw the same pose from various angles. Move around to do so, but always consider others when you do this.

6. Ask a clothed friend, relative or acquaintance to pose for you and draw the draped fabric. Drapery folds hold light and shadow and rely on the form underlying it.

You could also do this exercise without a model by simply setting up a still life with draped fabric.

7. Go back to abstract geometrical forms which for the pose, and shade in the areas carrying the body's weight.

8. Take your viewer and hold it in front of you so you can see the object you wish to draw. I usually close one eye to better direct what I am seeing, but you may wish to experiment and find what works for you. Focus on how you want to balance the figure, its grounding, and any other elements on the paper.

Practice this over and over with different figures and objects.

9. Or draw a few smaller frames on your paper. Newsprint suffices. Into these frames, begin to fit thumbnail sketches of the drawing object, employing different angles and perspectives.

10. Use your viewer to frame the figure you want to draw. Squint your eye to achieve better focus when doing so.

11. Start by drawing the negative space versus focusing on the figure. The figure arises from the negative space.

12. In a medium of your choice, draw outlines of geometric forms onto the page without shading them. Cover your page with them. Next, erase a few of them and draw them again, now overlapping some of the others on the page. Add a horizon line to the drawing. Observe how the forms appear to move through space with these steps.

13. Use the drawing you created in the first exercise and color it, remembering that the objects that are closest to the viewer are in sharper focus and more defined than the ones farther away. You can create this illusion by shading or coloring the closest objects darker than the ones that appear to recede into space.

14. Divide your page by drawing a horizontal line across it at approximately a third its height. Choose a point on the horizontal line.[7]

Any point will do, though it is easiest to focus on one approaching the mid-point of the horizontal line.

Next, draw lines that radiate in all directions from the vanishing point you just marked on your horizontal line. Now draw some simple boxes onto the page.

Note that drawing the boxes above the horizontal line means the viewer sees these objects from below, while anything place below the horizontal line means the viewer sees the objects from above.

Shade or color the boxes. As you spend time on this exercise, you might make it more fun by giving the boxes more identity. That could mean one of them turns into a house, another into a container or an old-fashioned tv set, yet another into a book and so on. Keep it simple.

---

[7] The horizontal line equates to eye level.

Spend time on this exercise so your brain remembers the activity and grasps the concept. Have fun!

15. Draw a cube in different perspectives under the same light source. Observe how doing so from different perspectives dramatically shifts values.

16. Draw the model's pose, the entire body, as geometric forms. In this case, do so via three-dimensional boxes. Draw how these boxes relate to one another. Shade them so plane changes become clear and obvious.

Materials to use: A graphite pencil, preferably light, or a carbon pencil or charcoal. Finer-grained or smooth paper.

17. Draw as many stick figures in an hour as you can to learn about proportions and get them right. Draw no flesh on the body's bones yet. Make sure the head is in proportion to the rest of the body.

18. Go to a park or a public place and observe the male, female, and child bodies passing you. Note their differences. After observing for at least 15 minutes, draw what you have seen from memory.

19. Use a pencil or a light medium for this exercise. Draw a cylinder moving back in space, then fill its form with coils and see how the form that comes toward you is bigger than its remainder that recedes in space.

20. Using geometrical abstraction for the arms or the legs of the figure, draw as you did in exercise number 1. Note the form closest to you and the viewer is larger than other portions of the form. What you see here requires a basic understanding of anatomy to realistically and believably render the forms.

When drawing a limb, foreshortened or not, of a figure, always start at the point where the limb connects to the body, then go outward. Otherwise your drawing's proportions will be off and look strange.

21. Draw a figure seated on the ground with the legs coming toward you. In this exercise, put down a ground plane the figure sits on. Something grid-like is best here. Observe how this grounding gives you an excellent sense about how the figure occupies space.

Again, start with abstract shapes for the legs and the feet and begin your coiled shading of the limbs at the point at which they meet the body.

The park, the symphony, the ballet, and many, many other public spaces are wonderful venues for gestural drawings. Choose one of them, your sketchbook and pencil or ink pen at the ready. Find a space to sit or stand and draw. First observe your surroundings for a few minutes, then draw simple representations of persons walking by or twisting, turning, or bending.

22. Draw at least thirty to forty quick gestures no longer than 30-seconds each. You are likely to find that you must draw quickly to capture the poses because your "models" here are not posing for you.

23. Draw a pose with the dynamics of movement in it. For example, a runner ready to start a sprint. Even though you may think about that position as stationary and non-moving, the tensed muscles are ready to spring into action. You can feel the movement, although it has not yet happened. Focus on the gesture only.

24. Draw the energetic flow of the body's rhythm in simple lines without details and with economy.

25. In this drawing exercise, break the body's forms down into their geometrical equivalents. Think of boxes, spheres, cubes, and cylinders. Shade each of these forms to create depth.

26. You can also draw these forms individually, then shade them. In other words, you draw a box, for example, and shade it.

27. Stand or sit with your pencil or ink pen with a starting point of your choosing on your paper. Relax your shoulders. Now look at the model and without looking at your paper, trace the contour of the figure. Continue until the contour is complete, then look at your drawing. The drawing may look strange to you. Please don't worry about that.

28. Practice blind contour drawing with different poses or with objects, your own hands or feet, and so on.

29. While blind contour informs about your ability to see, you may also draw the model's contour by looking at your paper once in a while.

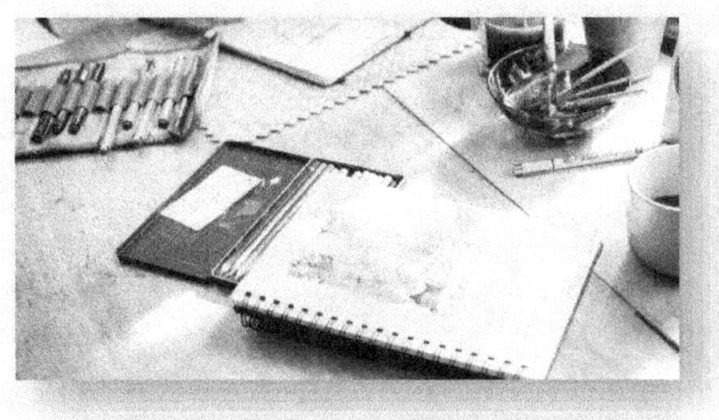

Bonus Section

Settings and Materials

Important Considerations to Succeed at Drawing follow in this short section. It is an introduction to figure drawing settings and to art materials. It is hardly comprehensive and intended to invite the artists reading this book to experiment and investigate further. I am only providing a few choice items for artists to consider. This book's accompanying **Workbook** contains many more drawing exercises, and an expanded section about settings and materials for figure drawing artists.

For now, here is the short-form version.

The stage/platform

If you are lucky enough to have a live model, either in a class setting or a private setting, the model must be on a platform so you can view the entire figure without losing it. If you take an online class, those that sprang up in force during the pandemic, find a class with a facilitator or instructor who knows this important piece of posing a model. The facilitator's camera must be able to accommodate the platform, different angles and perspectives of it, and so on.

Lighting

The above also applies to lighting. Lighting is an art all on its own. It can help or hinder your drawing. Make sure to use a spotlight on the model, not a flood light.

When lighting the human figure, the model, these are the options:

- Lighting from above creates a fairly even distribution of shadows and highlights.
- Lighting from the front flattens.
- Lighting from the left throws the right side of the figure into shadow.
- Lighting from the right throws the left side of the figure into shadow.
- Lighting from behind emphasizes the silhouette. It lends ambiguity.

The Model

The model brings a live, three-dimensional body with attitude, beauty, and idiosyncrasies.

The flesh of the body moves differently on skinny or fat people. Skinny models allow artists to see parts of the skeleton underlying the body. On hefty models, that is much harder and sometimes impossible to see. In either case, the study of anatomy and the muscles in your spare time enables you to draw either body type. Note also that drawing a skinny model can be quite challenging.

Tautness, muscularity, underlying structure, weight, weightiness, and weight distribution all inform what you see. How flesh moves comprises an inner and an outer component, both of which lend attitude.

An instructor who knows how to direct a model is valuable, and yes, the model earns his or her stipend with such an instructor. A great instructor directs a model to pose according to whatever specific teaching aims. These may include foreshortening, light and shadow work, work on specific body parts, long poses, short poses, and the list goes on.

A great model is one trained in all these aspects and one responsive to the instructor's work requests. Many such models understand movement quite well. They may be dancers in their regular profession.

Students owe the model respect and even gratitude.

Standing or sitting to draw

Both work well, but there are distinct differences that affect the drawing. In either case, make sure you are close to the model, your materials are ready, your body is relaxed, and distractions are gone, or at a minimum. No cell phones, no chatting with classmates and the like.

Easels

I like working at an easel to draw because standing at an easel provides me the perspective I most appreciate. It also demands my full attention when drawing.

Perhaps even more importantly, standing at an easel and drawing requires my own body to coordinate and feel the pose of the model. Of course, you can also sit on a drawing stool, but your perspective and body coordination will be different. Experiment and find out what works for you.

To chat or to focus

You might find yourself in an environment which may work or not work for you, depending on the art class you attend.

I find that a *process* happens inside me when entering drawing mode. It happens inside me when I draw, and that process simultaneously translates to the paper. It's a mindset, a kind of internal set-up that lasts throughout the drawing session.

The model in front of me represents a physical presence that demands full attention. I often see slight movements in the model's skin that reinforce the living quality that I seek to translate, the many movements seen and unseen that happen in the body.

What I observe and see is the overall, but it is fed by innumerable other gestures that can only be intuited rather than fully *seen*. Intuition, of course, is a kind of seeing. Equally important is that everything I see and draw must go through my body first, through my perceptive organs.

All seeing is transformation. It is the alchemy of the processes of life. But how all this gets framed or composed makes a huge difference in what translates, what others relate to and see. This requires immense focus and trust. It may take many drawings to achieve. Hundreds of mediocre drawings often precede one great one.

What does all this have to do with the environment you find yourself in in class, in a drawing group, or elsewhere?

The drawing environment sets the tone. When draftsmen and -women chat, pay attention to their phones, etc., their concentration and focus suffer. This can also happen with some music choices. Many teachers understand this, and some artists do, while others don't. Wisely choose your environment for drawing and aim to respect fellow artists if drawing in a group.

As an aside, during the pandemic, I signed up for an online figure drawing class in which the music was so distracting and dissonant that I had to turn off the sound.

On-line Drawing Sessions

The pandemic isolated many of us from events, classes, and outings we were used to. Many events and get-togethers went virtual. While it was wonderful to have models appear on my computer screen, a few drawbacks reared their ugly heads.

One of them was sessions put on by unqualified facilitators who knew little or nothing about how to set up the space, the model, the camera, and the entire session. Most were private individuals versus actual art instructors.

Online figure drawing sessions also attracted men and women who had never modeled before then and knew nothing about modeling. Perhaps it was just an easy way to make a few extra dollars from home. Often these models posed in bizarre ways, feet cut off and all the rest. Just because someone is willing to undress does not mean they are worthwhile models.

Yet another drawback is that your computer screen shows you a model that is nothing close to life size. The screen reduces detail and frames the figure in a way that is unnatural.

Be aware of these possible drawbacks. Know that they affect how you draw and especially whether you will be fully engaged in the activity.

Nevertheless, there is value in online figure drawing sessions. They are accessible, low cost, and convenient. As long as you are aware of the pros and cons of them, they provide you with practice sessions with a life model you might otherwise lack.

Paper

Note that all materials you use to draw are connected to what the eye sees and they are tactile as well. Here are some options for exploring: newsprint, vellum, watercolor paper, charcoal paper, mylar, and colored paper.

All papers come in various sizes and have varied tooth. Tooth refers to the surface of the paper, whether it is smooth or rough. All produce different effects and affect how your pencil, charcoal, ink, or watercolor interact and reflect.

Experiment with different formats and materials to find what works best for you.

18x24 paper is the standard art class paper format and if you opt for it, make sure to use newsprint and higher quality drawing papers. Note that newsprint is a cheap paper that yellows and degrades over time. Archival quality papers, which are, are more expensive but certainly worth the expense.

Drawing media

Drawing media include charcoal, pen and ink, chalk, watercolors, pencils, including graphite and oil-based ones, crayons, and more. All of them have different qualities and uses. Make it your mission to learn how to use each of them.

A quick note: if you love charcoal like I do, have a couple of kneaded erasers handy. They work great to graduate shadows and put in subtle reflected light shades. Using them instead of white highlights will give your drawings a natural look.

Initially, use materials like pencil, pen and ink and charcoal instead of colors and paints. The reason is that the study of color is a lifelong endeavor and that color can easily mislead and distract from your drawing.

Again, experiment with materials until you find those right for you. Gradually add more if that is your desire.

That's it. Go draw the figure!

Selected Bibliography

"Anatomy and Drawing (Dover Art Instruction): Victor Perard.

"Basic Human Anatomy: An Essential Visual Guide for Artists: Osti, Roberto, Drake, Peter.

"Bridgman's Complete Guide to Drawing From Life: Bridgman, George B.

"Constructive Anatomy: Includes Nearly 500 Illustrations (Dover Anatomy for Artists): George B. Bridgman.

"Darwin and Facial Expression: A Century of Research in Review: Ekman, Paul.

"Drawing the Head and Hands: Loomis, Andrew.

"Emotion in the Human Face: Ekman, Paul.

"Figure Drawing Book by Nathan Goldstein."

"Heads, Features and Faces (Dover Anatomy for Artists): George B. Bridgman.

"Leonardo's Notebooks: Writing and Art of the Great Master (Notebook Series) - Kindle Edition by Da Vinci, Leonardo, Suh, H. Anna.

"Michelangelo: Divine Draftsman and Designer: Bambach, Carmen C., Barry, Claire M., Caglioti, Francesco, Elam, Caroline, Marongiu, Marcella, Mussolin, Mauro: 9781588396372: Amazon.Com: Books."

"Michelangelo Life Drawings – Dover Publications."

"Perspective Made Easy (Dover Art Instruction): Ernest R. Norling: 8601406979970: Amazon.Com: Books."

"Rey's Anatomy: Figurative Art Lessons From the Classroom: Bustos, Rey, Goldfinger, Eliot: 9781624650598: Amazon.Com: Books."

"Rudolf Arnheim: Art and Visual Perception - International Center of Photography."

"The Art Spirit by Robert Henri | Henri."

"The Artist's Guide to Human Anatomy (Dover Anatomy for Artists): Bammes, Gottfried: 9780486436418: Amazon.Com: Books.".

"The Complete Guide to Anatomy for Artists & Illustrators: Bammes, Gottfried: 9781782213581: Amazon.Com: Books."

"The Expression of the Emotions in Man and Animals (Penguin Classics): Darwin, Charles: 9780141439440: Amazon.Com: Books."

"The Genius of Leonardo Da Vinci: Vinci, Leonardo Da, Barber, Barrington, Vasari, Signor Giorgio: 9781398820593: Amazon.Com: Books."

"The Human Machine (Dover Anatomy for Artists): George B. Bridgman: 0800759227075: Amazon.Com: Books."

"The Natural Way to Draw: A Working Plan for Art Study: Nicolaides, Kimon: 9780395530078: Amazon.Com: Books."

"The Power of the Center: A Study of Composition in the Visual Arts Revised Edition | Rudolf Arnheim | 1st Printing.

Index

About the Author

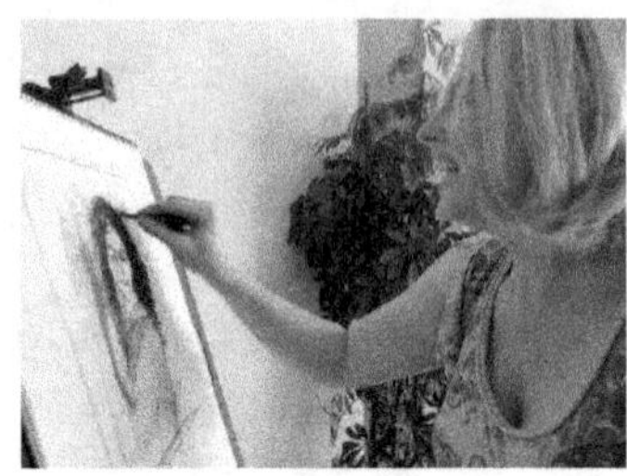

Gabrielle Dahms is a renaissance woman: artist, author, presenter, and entrepreneur. She holds a master's in history and loves to research and write. Her latest books, *Figure Drawing: Rhythm and Language of the Human Form* and its accompanying *Workbook impart* technical and artistic considerations and knowledge when drawing the human figure. The books cull teachings from over four decades of drawing the figure. —Her other non-fiction publications include the titles in *The Real Estate Investor Manuals* series, and hundreds of articles and blog posts about real estate. When away from the keyboard, she enjoys nature, travel, and other cultures. She also volunteers for local food banks and animal welfare causes.

3% of the proceeds of this book support the arts and artistic expression through inception of a Foundation. Find out more as the Foundation gets up and running.

www.ingramcontent.com/pod-product-compliance
Lightning Source LLC
Chambersburg PA
CBHW052006150726
47999CB00004B/1545